Bible Study Guide and Workbook for Women

A Guided Journey Through Scripture with Reflection Prompts, Practical Lessons, and Weekly Devotionals to Deepen Your Relationship with God

Welcome Aboard, Check Out This Limited-Time Free Bonus!

Ahoy, reader! Welcome to the Ahoy Publications family, and thanks for snagging a copy of this book! Since you've chosen to join us on this journey, we'd like to offer you something special.

Check out the link below for a FREE e-book filled with delightful facts about American History.

But that's not all - you'll also have access to our exclusive email list with even more free e-books and insider knowledge. Well, what are ye waiting for? Click the link below to join and set sail toward exciting adventures in American History.

Access your bonus here
https://ahoypublications.com/
Or, Scan the QR code!

Table of Contents

Part 1: Bible Study Guide for Women

Grow Your Faith with Inspiring Women of the Bible and Practical Lessons

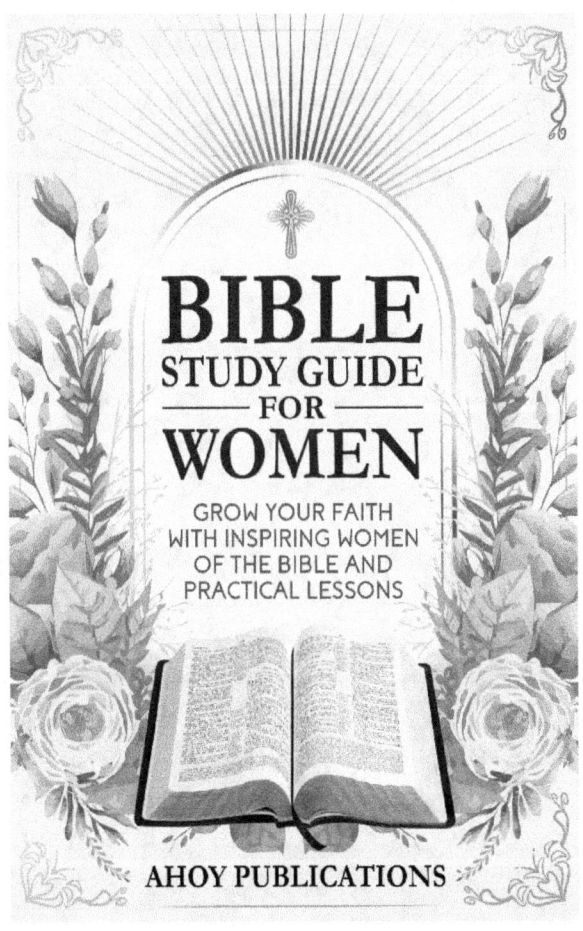

Introduction

Are you seeking a way to deepen your faith and spiritual understanding of God's Word, especially as a woman? The Bible Study Guide for Women is here to help. This book is written with you in mind. It focuses on the parts most relevant to women through Bible verses and prayers speaking directly to a woman's heart. If you want a book to help you connect deeply with the Bible, look no further.

This guide is the empowerment you need to become a better version of yourself, from teaching you how to study the Bible to helping you discover your God-given purpose. It gives you easy-to-follow techniques on how to approach the Bible – and gives tips on how to prepare before you start reading. These techniques help you feel more confident and ready to understand what you read.

Women have been important to God's work from the beginning of time to today. The Bible is full of stories about strong, faithful women who played essential roles in God's plan, and their stories inspire you to live out your faith with the same strength and trust in God. This guide features several godly women and looks closer at their lives through a character-study technique. You can learn from their experiences and find inspiration in their faith and courage.

The Bible Study Guide for Women makes the Bible easier to understand by breaking it into smaller sections. Sometimes, when studying the Bible, knowing where to start or how to find the parts that matter most to you can be overwhelming. This guide solves this problem by dividing the Bible into sections, including easy-to-follow lessons. Each section is carefully chosen and written in a way you can resonate with.

This guide offers journaling prompts for personal reflection at the end of each chapter. Writing down your thoughts helps you process what you've read and makes remembering and acting on the lessons easier. These prompts encourage you to think about what you learned and how it applies to your life. They let you talk to God through writing.

If you're ready to start a new chapter in your spiritual journey, the Bible Study Guide for Women is the perfect companion to help you. Start reading today and discover how this guide can transform your understanding of the Bible and help you grow in your faith.

Chapter 1: How to Prepare for Bible Study

The Bible is a collection of God's written word for believers to gain deeper knowledge and understanding of God. It's not only one book. It is a collection of many books written by several people over centuries and generations.

You can compare the Bible to an ancient library. Picture yourself walking into a gigantic library full of old books with immense wisdom. On the shelves, you find books telling different stories: stories about the history of a group of people. Some are about laws. Some are poetry or wise sayings, and others are the biographies of influential people in the history of Christianity. This is the Bible – a library of books centuries apart written by several people with a definite style and purpose under the Holy Spirit's inspiration.

You can compare the Bible to an ancient library.[1]

Every believer is a scholar in the school of the spirit. Like how you must read textbooks, journals, and other relevant material to maintain your studies or career choice – it is the same with reading the Bible and the school of the spirit. The Bible is a book you cannot just read without studying, especially as a woman.

This first chapter focuses on equipping you with practical and spiritual tools to effectively prepare for Bible study, emphasizing the importance of creating a conducive environment, setting intentions, and introducing Bible study methods to help you make the most of your study session.

What Is Bible Study?

Bible study is like pausing from the rush of life to sit down with your pen, notepad, and Bible and learn from the deep things of God through the help of the Holy Spirit. The ultimate goal of studying the Bible is not to say you have read the bible cover to cover. Instead, it is to know God more profoundly.

As a woman, there's something special about opening the Bible, reading, thinking, and understanding what it says. Life can get extremely busy, with many things pulling women in different directions—work, family, etc. However, sitting down with the Bible is akin to taking a moment to breathe, listen, and learn what can potentially shape how you see the world and react to life's issues.

When you start a Bible study, it's like sitting down with a wise friend with many stories to tell and advice to give. This wise friend is none other than the Bible. When you commit to studying the Bible, you are guided by faith and wisdom passed down for thousands of years.

Do you remember Peter, Jesus' disciple? Remember how when he became afraid of the sea, he began to drown. Fear can drown destinies. It is usually the fear of failure that causes most people to fail. The cure of fear is faith. One of the easiest ways to build your faith is by studying the word of God. The Bible says in Romans 10:16-17, "But not all the Israelites accepted the good news. For Isaiah says, "Lord, who has believed our message? Consequently, faith comes from hearing the message, which is heard through the word about Christ."

Bible Study is not a one-time thing. It is the main source of spiritual growth for the believer. You cannot ignore the word of God and sustain relevance over a long period. The word keeps you updated with God's mind for his people daily. Remember, God speaks to His people expressly through His word.

The Importance of Preparation for Bible Study

Bible study is not only about picking up the Bible when you feel guilty for not opening it for months. That's no way to study. You are only deceiving yourself if that is your motivation to read God's Word. The Bible says in Galatians 6:7-8, *"Do not be deceived: God cannot be mocked. A man reaps what he sows. Whoever sows to please their flesh, from the flesh will reap destruction; whoever sows to please the Spirit, from the Spirit will reap eternal life."*

Studying the Bible is serious business; therefore, it requires proper physical and spiritual preparation. If you haven't guessed it already, studying the Bible after spiritually preparing your heart is one way to sow to please the spirit. As the scripture above states, you are well on your way to securing eternal life for choosing this path.

When you prepare, your mind is ready to learn. You focus more, understand more, and easily remember what you read. Preparing your mind and heart before studying is vital to getting the most out of Bible study. It leads to spiritual growth, personal development, and strong community bonds.

Spiritual Growth

Spiritual growth is one of the most essential reasons to prepare for Bible study. When you take time to prepare, you open your heart and mind to God. As you study, you learn more about God and His love for you. The Bible is full of stories and teachings showing how much God cares for you. When you prepare, you can better focus on these lessons and understand them more deeply. It helps your spirit grow stronger because you fill your heart with God's truth and love. You grow spiritually with each session, making you feel closer to God and giving you peace and strength daily.

Personal Development

All that pertains to life and godliness has been made available to believers through the word of God. Diverse stories and admonishments in the Bible teach people to be kind, honest, diligent, and compassionate. Everything you need to live a good and fulfilling life is within the pages of God's Word. These lessons are too important to be approached casually. Hence, preparation is necessary. As you read and understand the Bible, you will see how these lessons apply to your life. You might notice areas where you can improve, like being more patient or forgiving. Before you know it, these small changes lead to a massive upgrade in your character, turning you into the virtuous woman described in Proverbs 31: 1-31. You become the best version of yourself, the person God wants you to be.

Community Building

Preparation before Bible study, whether alone or with a group of women with the same vision, cannot be overemphasized. The more prepared each person is, the more interactive and fulfilling the study session. Every group member will come from a place of readiness and openness to learn from each other's insight inspired by God's spirit. Growth is inevitable, personally and communally.

The Power of Specific Goals

During your preparation, remember to make specific goals. You will need it. A specific goal when studying is like picking out the blue color in the sea of navy blue, sky blue, and ocean blue colors. Although they are all in the family of blue, if your goal is to get the ocean blue, you will naturally strive to make the selection. Right? Picking a different color or a color at random will not be as fulfilling because a goal is already in place. Your specific goal in Bible study could be understanding a scripture, finding peace, or picking out a biblical principle to apply to your life.

The Bible is full of wisdom and insight. So, to make the most of your Bible study session for however long it would be, biting small chunks so you can chew and digest without issues is advisable.

Specific goals will help you study better. For example, if your goal is to understand a topic like honesty, concentrating on Bible verses and stories that make the topic easy to understand will give you a direction to follow and stay focused.

Specific goals will help you study better.'

Besides providing definite direction, goals help you track your spiritual growth. If your goal is to pray or trust God more, you can see how well you are doing over time. Goals help you stay committed and motivated. You feel closer to God and stronger in your faith as you meet your goals.

The Need for Spiritual Preparation

Bible study is no funfair. Studying the Bible without spiritual preparation is the worst way to study. It's like jumping into a swimming pool, and you come out completely dry after spending hours in it. Not even the hair on your skin is wet. That would have been a miracle in a different circumstance. However, in this context, the swimming pool is the Bible, and coming out dry is not good. It means there is no deep understanding.

This is why people still struggle with spiritual growth, even though they can read the Bible cover to cover in various translations.

What does it mean to prepare spiritually for Bible study? It invites the Spirit of God's presence to join you for the study session. As the spirit leads, you could take it up a notch by fasting before and during your study time.

In John 14:26, Jesus said, *"But the Advocate, the Holy Spirit, whom the Father will send in my name, will teach you all things and will remind you of everything I have said to you."* The Holy Spirit is the believers' access to the deep things of God, 1 Cor. 2:9-10, *"However, as it is written: "What no eye has seen, what no ear has heard, and what no human mind has conceived"— the things God has prepared for those who love him— these are the things God has revealed to us by his Spirit. The Spirit searches all things, even the deep things of God."*

It is the Spirit that alerts you to moments in a Bible story. The Bible is full of mysteries and keys to succeeding in all facets of life.

Redemption without empowerment leads to frustration. The agent of empowerment is the Holy Spirit. The channel through which the empowerment comes is the word of God. Your hunger and thirst are the price to pay for this empowerment through studying the word. Psalms 63:1. Your thirst for God's knowledge and wisdom lies beneath the letters printed on the Bible's pages, giving you access to the power backing God's Word.

So, even though you can pick up your Bible and read until you get tired or sleepy, it doesn't determine if your faith has increased. It is not the length of time spent or the number of Bible stories you read that increases your faith in God's Word. No. Don't be fooled! The light you encounter from God's word increases your faith. This light comes from the enlightenment of your spirit and the eyes of your understanding being open.

This is why Paul, praying for the Church, said in Ephesians 1:17-18:

"That the God of our Lord Jesus Christ, the Father of glory, may give to you the spirit of wisdom and revelation in the knowledge of Him, the eyes of your understanding being enlightened; that you may know what is the hope of His calling, what are the riches of the glory of His inheritance in the saints..."

Practical Preparation for Your Bible Study Session

As you prepare spiritually, you must also prepare practically. Pick a quiet place to focus on reading the Bible without interruption. It could be your bedroom, a cozy corner of your home, or a spot outside where you feel peaceful. Choosing a time when you won't be distracted is important, perhaps early in the morning before your day starts or in the evening after everything has settled down so you can concentrate better and avoid distractions.

Next, ensure you have everything before you start studying. Of course, you'll need your Bible. A notebook and a pen are also essential. The notebook is for writing down thoughts, questions, or important points that come to mind while reading. A Bible study session without these tools is like farming without a hoe and a machete. Having them close ensures you don't have to cut your concentration to look for anything.

Take your time with each verse. If you come across a word or phrase you don't understand, don't worry. You can look it up later or re-read it to see if it makes more sense. Mentally prepare yourself to read and study until you get insight.

Bible Study Techniques

You can employ simple Bible study techniques to help you truly understand the Bible and make the most of your study time. Some are:

- Inductive Bible study
- Topical Bible study
- Character study

The inductive Bible study technique involves observing Bible passages and drawing conclusions. This Bible study technique aims to answer six (6) questions.

1. Who is speaking in the Bible passage?
2. When is the event taking place?
3. Where is the event taking place?
4. What is the Bible passage about?
5. Why is the message from that scripture relevant?
6. How does the message apply in your life?

The character study technique is another great way to study the Bible. It focuses on a particular character in the Bible and how they became living testimonies of God's faithfulness. This book is mainly based on character study. You will learn about women in the Bible and their relationship with God. For effective character study, here are steps to follow:

1. Select a biblical character.
2. Search the scriptures for relevant verses about them.
3. Use tools like Bible dictionaries and anointed books to learn more about the character.
4. Determine how you can apply the lessons in your life.

The last study technique is the topical study technique. Like its name, this technique explores topics or concepts in the Bible. The topical study technique requires you to:

1. Select a topic.
2. Research the topic.
3. Select relevant Bible verses to study.
4. Ask questions and summarize your conclusions.
5. Write a journal on how you intend to apply the knowledge you gathered.

Here are tips on how to read and annotate scripture, keep notes, and use a journal:

- Start with a prayer. Before you open your Bible to study, take time to pray. Ask God to help you understand His word and teach you. This prayer can go a long way. According to John 14:26, the Holy Spirit is there to teach.

- Go slow and steady. There is no need to rush. You can pick one scripture, maybe only a few verses, and read slowly. Keep reading and re-reading until you understand what is said.

- As you read, if a part of the scripture catches your attention, use a pencil or highlighter to mark or underline the verse. It will help you remember it easily. Also, the verse becomes easy to pick out when you open your Bible.

- After you read a verse, meditate on it and make notes. There is no need to write too much, just a few words to remind you. Psalm 1:2-3 says, *"...but whose delight is in the law of the Lord, and who meditates on his law day and night. That person is like a tree planted by streams of water, which yields its fruit in season and whose leaf does not wither—whatever they do prospers."* Meditation causes the light of God's Word to shine brighter. This is why God told Joshua in Joshua 1:8 to meditate on the word day and night.

- Don't be afraid to ask questions. When you read and find parts difficult to understand, don't ignore them or make assumptions. Write down your questions. You can ask someone more spiritually mature or pray for better understanding. The Holy Spirit is there to help. Ask, and you shall receive, including knowledge and understanding.

- Get a journal that you can use daily or weekly, depending on your study schedule. One is enough. When it's full, don't discard it. Get a new one and keep the old one for reference purposes.

Documenting your daily finds in a journal will help your progress.[3]

- After reading and writing, reflect on what you read and pray again. Say a prayer of thanksgiving and ask the Lord to help you apply the knowledge. Luke 6:47—48, *"As for everyone who comes to me and hears my words and puts them into practice, I will show you what they are like. They are like a man building a house who dug down deep and laid the foundation on rock. When a flood came, the torrent struck that house but could not shake it because it was well built."*

Bible Study Challenges for Women

Like every rewarding and fulfilling activity, Bible study also has challenges. These challenges differ for each person. Here are common Bible study challenges women face:

- **Difficulty Creating Study Schedules:** Women usually face challenges balancing Bible study with responsibilities like work, family, and household tasks. There is almost no time to spare once they complete their daily tasks. It poses a huge challenge for them. Some women postpone their study sessions to ensure they get everything else done.

- **Difficulty Maintaining Your Initial Zeal to Study the Bible:** Building a consistent and regular Bible study habit will test you in several ways, especially when life gets busy or motivation wanes.

- **Experiencing Spiritual Dryness:** There are times when studying the Bible might feel stressful. An activity that should have been fulfilling now feels like one you should have left for another time because you can't 'feel it.'

- **Distractions When It's Time to Study:** As a woman, especially one who loves God enough to fellowship with Him through His word, distractions will likely come from every angle. Distractions could be notifications, kids, family members, or intrusive thoughts, all aiming to throw you off the path of knowledge.

- **Trying to Put What You've Learned to Work:** After studying the Bible, many people are blessed with great knowledge and understanding. However, applying this knowledge becomes a problem. Proverbs 4:7 explains how wisdom is the principal. What is wisdom? Wisdom is applied knowledge. So, getting knowledge is not enough if you don't apply it. Even Jesus talks about people who receive the word but cannot do anything with it – Matthew 13:20-22.

How to Tackle These Challenges

Tackling the Challenge of Creating Time:

- **Be Intentional About Your Time:** You can set aside a specific time each day, even if it's only 10-15 minutes, for Bible study. Little doses every day will help you prepare your mind and body for longer sessions.

- **Make Studying the Bible a Daily Routine:** You don't have to wait until you are completely free. You can read a verse or a devotional while having breakfast or during a break at work.

Tackling the Challenge of Staying Consistent

- **Don't Raise the Bar Too High:** Be realistic. Start with small, manageable goals, like reading one chapter or a few verses a day. It is your study time. You're not studying for an exam or to win an award. Take your time.

- **You Know Yourself Better Than Anyone:** If staying consistent is an issue, try pairing up with a study partner or joining a group for accountability. This way, you will always be encouraged and encourage others to stay on track.

Tackling the Challenge of Spiritual Dryness

- **Try Different Bible Study Approaches:** Pick a topic and explore. If it becomes boring, switch to character study and study about one person or a group of people in the Bible. If this still doesn't do it for you, pick a random book of the Bible to study and make notes in a journal. One of these methods will get you hooked, at least for a reasonable period.

- **Ask God:** Pray for a fresh perspective and the desire to learn more about Him. This is the ultimate cure for spiritual dryness. The moment you involve the mystery of asking God for more of Him through the word, the Holy Spirit will appear to carry you deeper into the depths of God's wisdom and knowledge in His word.

Tackling the Challenge of Distractions

- **You Are Allowed to Have Some "Me Time.":** Use it. Don't feel guilty about wanting alone time where it's only you, your Bible, and the Holy Spirit. Find a place where you can focus without interruptions.

- **Set Boundaries:** Everyone who wants to communicate with you can wait a few minutes or hours. Turn off your phone! If you feel that is too extreme, silence your phone or set it to "Do Not Disturb" mode during study time. Ultimately, you are building someone they would be proud to be around. You need your study time for your well-being.

Tackling the Challenge of Applying the Knowledge

- After reading, spend a few minutes thinking about how you can apply what you've learned. Believers are admonished in James 1:22, "Do not merely listen to the word, and so deceive yourselves. Do what it says."

- Write down insights that stand out, meditate on them, and how to apply them in your daily life.

Inspiring Anecdotes from Women and How Studying the Bible Enhanced Their Lives and Relationship with God

Beth Moore | Author

"The scriptures have been a source of strength and guidance in my personal life. As a Bible teacher and author, studying the Bible has helped me navigate challenging times and brought me even closer to God."

Lysa TerKeurst | President of Proverbs 31 Ministries

"Studying the Bible changed my life completely. It has helped me find peace, purpose, and healing."

Joyce Meyer | Christian Author and Speaker

"Studying God's Word has helped me understand God's love and forgiveness. It gave me hope, improved my personal and spiritual growth, and guided me to start my ministry."

Journaling Prompt

Create your first journal entry by affirming your goals for Bible study. What do you want to learn, apply, and achieve?

Chapter 2: The Women of Genesis

The Book of Genesis is the first book of the Bible, written by the prophet Moses under the inspiration of the Spirit of God. It is one of the oldest books of the Bible with many interesting and inspiring stories, such as the story of creation, Noah and the ark, the story of Abraham, Joseph and his coat of many colors, Isaac and his well, Sodom and Gomorrah, Jacob, and his multi-colored flock, and many more.

The Book of Genesis is the first book of the Bible.'

In this chapter, you will study the lives of a few Biblical characters. It focuses on the women of Genesis – Adam's wife, Eve, in the story of creation; Abraham's wife, Sarah; Sarah's handmaid, Hagar; Isaac's wife, Rebekah; and Laban's two daughters, Leah and Rachel.

These women experienced specific challenges that tested their faith and trust in God. Each responded uniquely. This chapter explores how they handled their situations and came out victorious. You can learn many lessons from the women of Genesis. So, grab your pen and notebook.

Eve | The First Woman of Creation

Often referred to as the mother of all living, Eve was Adam's missing rib. She was created as a help-meet for Adam, as his companion, so they could carry out God's purpose for their lives. During their time in the Garden of Eden, they had everything they needed. They were at peace, and their days were filled with joy and laughter, without pain or fear, and in God's presence. They had dominion over all things created by God.

God gave the couple one command: not to eat from the tree of the knowledge of good and evil. It stood in the middle of the garden like a shiny toy, and like every forbidden thing, it had fruits more beautiful and enticing than the rest. Eve never questioned the command, trusting in God's wisdom.

Unfortunately, the serpent used his subtle and deceptive nature to take advantage of her innocence and naivety. It convinced her they would not die as God told them, but their eyes would be open, and they would become like gods (Genesis 3:5). If only she knew that the serpent's agenda was to make them lose their place in God's kingdom. Eve ate the fruit and quickly shared her newest discovery with her husband.

They indeed became gods. However, God sent them out of the garden before they would eat of the Tree of Life and become immortals, and they rebelled against God as the angel Lucifer (the serpent) had done. In His anger at their disobedience, he humbled them by allowing them to work for their food, but He never took away their godly nature. In Psalm 82:6-7 God said:

> *"I said, 'You are "gods;" you are all sons of the Most High.'*
> *But you will die like mere mortals; you will fall like every*
> *other ruler."*

Eve was an open-minded woman, an optimist, and an excellent communicator. She had faith in God and was intrigued to see and hear a serpent talk. However, Eve's curiosity got the best of her, and she took the fruit. Her life became a testimony to the consequences of disobedience and the unending grace of God.

Sarah | The Mother of Nations

Being told you would be a mother of nations yet remaining barren for over 80 years is not something many women could handle. Sarah married Abraham when he was known as Abram and lived in his father's house. Their journey together was difficult, but she had faith in God and loved her husband dearly.

When God called Abraham to leave his father's house in Ur, it surprised Sarah because she had never known life outside her family and friends. However, instead of bombarding her husband with questions, she trusted him and believed in God, who spoke to him. They packed their belongings and began their long journey to a land they had never seen before.

After many years of trying to conceive, Sarah offered her handmaid to her husband so he could at least have an heir. However, it did not end well. Hagar, her handmaid, looked down on Sarah when she bore Abraham a son. Sarah became bitter and cried out to God.

Even in her moments of doubt, Sarah never stopped believing in God. She was almost 90 years old when God kept His promise. He sent angels, and when they visited the small family, they told Abraham that Sarah would soon give birth to a son. Sarah laughed when she heard it. She thought, 'How can I carry a child at this age,' to which the angels replied, "Is anything too hard for the Lord?"

True to His word, God gave her Isaac less than a year after the angels' visit. God, in His sense of humor, asked them to name the child Isaac in Genesis 17:19:

> *"Then God said, "Yes, but your wife Sarah will bear you a son, and you will call him Isaac. I will establish my covenant with him as an everlasting covenant for his descendants after him."*

Isaac means 'laughter,' and Sarah laughed when the angels visited.

When Isaac was born, Sarah told the people the Lord had made her laugh after so many years in Genesis 21:6, "Sarah said, *"God has brought me laughter, and everyone who hears about this will laugh with me."* He is indeed faithful.

The almighty test of faith came after many years of his birth: the sacrifice of their promised child. Sarah looked at her husband and saw his unwavering faith, so she let the child go. Sarah understood that faith is not always easy, and faith is trusting God, especially when you do not understand His ways.

The Bible says in Isaiah 55:8-9:

> *"For my thoughts are not your thoughts, neither are your ways my ways," declares the Lord. "As the heavens are higher than the earth, so are my ways higher than your ways and my thoughts than your thoughts."*

In Jeremiah 29:11, believers are assured of what to expect from God and why they should stand firm in faith.

"For I know the plans I have for you," declares the Lord, "plans to prosper you and not to harm you, plans to give you hope and a future."

This is why Sarah stood firm in her faith. Hebrews 11:11 testifies of Sarah:

> *"And by faith, even Sarah, who was past childbearing age, was enabled to bear children because she considered him faithful who had made the promise."*

As a wife, Sarah did her best to support Abraham. She cared for her household, cooked meals, and ensured their servants were well-fed and cared for. She was the queen of Abraham's kingdom. Sarah's story inspires others to trust God, no matter how impossible things seem, because nothing is too hard for the Lord.

Hagar | Mother of the Ishmaelites

Hagar was Sarah's servant and Ishmael's mother. Her story begins when she becomes a servant in the house of Abraham and Sarah. She had to learn to adapt to their ways, to serve her master and his wife faithfully.

Hagar's life was without drama until Sarah approached her with a strange proposal. Sarah asked her to lie with her husband, Abraham, so that she could bear him a child. Hagar was surprised at the request but had no choice as a servant. She became pregnant with Abraham's first child.

This new status got into her head, and she became proud. She forgot her place and was soon displaced. Sarah complained about her attitude, and Abraham told Sarah to deal with her as she pleased. When Hagar couldn't take the punishment anymore, she ran away. She encountered an angel in the wilderness who advised her to return to her mistress, Sarah (Genesis 16:6-16).

Hagar encountered an angel who advised her to return to her mistress, Sarah.[5]

The angel told her to submit to Sarah and that God would multiply her seed. He assured her that God had seen her secret tears and would help her and her son. Her encounter with God in the wilderness caused her to have faith in Him. She obeyed His voice and went back to Sarah. Hagar acknowledged that God sees all. She called Him "El Roi," the God who sees me.

Not long after she returned to her mistress, she bore Abraham a son and called him Ishmael as the Lord commanded. Fast forward to Isaac's birth, and everything changed again. During the great feast, Abraham organized for his newborn son, Sarah caught Hagar's son mocking the child, and her anger flared.

Sarah demanded that Abraham send Hagar and her son away, but he hesitated until God asked him to listen to Sarah and assured him that He would watch over the child. After all, the child of the promise was Isaac and not Ishmael. Abraham packed food and water for Hagar and sent them away like he was told (Genesis 21:12-14).

As the duo wandered in the wilderness of Beersheba, they ran out of water, and Hagar left the boy under a tree, saying in her heart, 'I don't want to see him die.' While she wept, the boy also wept. God heard the child's cry and spoke to Hagar: Genesis 21:17-20:

> *"God heard the boy crying, and the angel of God called to Hagar from heaven and said to her, "What is the matter, Hagar? Do not be afraid; God has heard the boy crying as he lies there. Lift the boy up and take him by the hand, for I will make him into a great nation."*

Then God opened her eyes, and she saw a well of water. So, she went and filled the skin with water and gave the boy a drink. God was with the boy as he grew up. He lived in the desert and became an archer."

Hagar raised her boy in the wilderness, trusting that God would be with them all their lives. He had promised that Ishmael would become a great nation, and she held onto that promise. She learned to trust in God and believe in His promises and was not put to shame.

Rebekah | The Mother of Israel

Abraham didn't want his son, Isaac, to marry anyone from the Canaanites where they were living because they didn't follow God's ways. So, he called his trusted servant and made him swear to go back to his homeland, to Abraham's relatives, to find a wife for Isaac.

Rebekah was an answered prayer for Isaac. The servant sent to find him a wife prayed to God to guide him and show him the right woman for his master's son by a sign. In his prayer, he told God that the right woman should be willing to give him some water and be kind enough to draw water for his camels.

While the servant was praying, God sent Rebekah his way. She did everything he asked God for with a smile on her face. The servant was shocked at how fast God answered his prayer. The servant asked to meet with her family, and Rebekah, led by the Spirit, didn't hesitate to take him to her family. She had heard stories of how God led His people and knew this was God's work.

When Abraham's servant told her family about the purpose of his visit and how God had led him to her, Rebekah didn't hesitate. Her family wanted her to stay a few more days, but when they asked her if she would go with the servant, she said, "I will go." This was a big step of faith, leaving everything she knew and trusting God's plan for her life.

Rebekah heard a call from God and did not question or delay. She immediately acted, trusting that God knew best. Rebekkah's faith was tested when she became Isaac's wife. She was barren for many years. Childlessness was seen as a curse in those days and could bring great shame to a woman. However, Rebekah continued to trust in God.

After twenty years of waiting, God answered their prayers, and she conceived twins. While pregnant, she made a prayer of inquiry about the children. God told her two nations were in her womb – the older would serve the younger. When the time came for the blessing of her sons, Jacob and Esau, Rebekah knew she had a role to play.

She remembered God's promise that the older son, Esau, would serve the younger son, Jacob. So, she took a bold step to ensure Jacob received the blessing. Some might say she was deceptive, but in her heart, she aligned with God's Word about Jacob being the chosen one. Her actions ensured God's will was fulfilled. Genesis 27:6-30

Her faith was proactive. She was willing to take risks for what she believed to be God's plan. Rebekah trusted God wholeheartedly. She was willing to step out in faith, leave her comfort zone, and make hard decisions to stay aligned with God's plan and purpose.

Leah | The First-Born Daughter

Leah was the elder daughter of Laban, Jacob's uncle. Upon reaching his mother's homeland, Jacob met Leah's younger sister, Rachel, and agreed to work for Laban for seven years to marry her. However, Laban deceived Jacob on the wedding night. He was given Leah instead of Rachel. Laban's people had a custom where the younger daughter could not be married before the elder ones. So, Jacob had a wife he did not love. When he discovered he had married Leah, he was sad Laban didn't tell him about their custom. However, Leah was now his wife, and he couldn't change that.

Laban saw his zeal to marry his second daughter, Rachel, and asked for another seven years of service from Jacob. He gladly agreed. Leah always knew that Jacob didn't love her, but instead of giving up on her marriage, she held on and trusted in God to keep her in her husband's house. She refused to be bitter. God saw her heart and that she was unloved and opened her womb.

While Rachel was still barren, Leah had given Jacob six sons and a daughter, Reuben, Simeon, Levi, Judah, Issachar, Zebulun, and Dinah (Genesis 29 and Genesis 30). After her fourth son, she prayed to God for more children. God answered her prayer (Genesis 30:17). Jacob's heart was still with Rachel, and she had not yet given him a child.

God made Leah so fruitful because He saw she had so much faith in Him. She sought His intervention in her marriage, and He blessed her with many children. Psalm 127:3 says, *"Children are a heritage from the Lord, offspring a reward from him."*

By the time Leah gave birth to her fourth child, Judah, she was no longer feeling rejected. Instead, she said, *"This time I will praise the Lord"* (Genesis 29:35). She decided to focus on God and praise Him for establishing her place in her husband's house. Leah displayed her faith in God by seeking and praising Him despite facing rejection from her husband. She continued to fulfill her role as a wife and mother.

Leah was not the preferred wife, but God honored her in many ways. Leah was the mother of six of Jacob's twelve sons (the twelve tribes of Israel), and her son, whom she named Judah (praise), was the ancestor of King David, the lineage of Jesus Christ. She found her value and purpose in Him. Her faithfulness to God led to a legacy far greater than she could have imagined.

Leah gave birth to Judah, who is Jesus' ancestor.'

Rachel | Jacob's Love at First Sight

Jacob served Laban for fourteen years so that he could marry Rachel. She was highly favored (Genesis 29:17). When Jacob arrived at the well where she came to draw water, he rolled away the stone from the well's mouth and helped her water her father's sheep. She enamored him. Seeing a woman tend to sheep was new to him. Jacob immediately fell in love with her – it was evident in how he spoke and looked at her.

Laban had given him a condition: Jacob must serve him for seven years in exchange for Rachel's hand in marriage. Seven long years! However, it didn't deter the young man. In what felt like a month, the seven years were over. Jacob was excited to receive the love of his life. Genesis 29:20 says:

"So Jacob served seven years to get Rachel, but they seemed like only a few days to him because of his love for her."

However, when the time came for their marriage, Rachel was told to step back and allow her sister Leah to marry Jacob because of their custom. Imagine how Rachel felt, watching the man she loved marry another because of customs, unable to warn him beforehand. Rachel's heart broke, but she had to listen to her father. Neither she nor her sister, Leah, had any choice.

Jacob was relentless. He agreed to work another seven years for her, and Rachel couldn't have been happier. She felt bad for her sister, but Jacob's love was strong. She had to share him with Leah when she finally became his wife. Leah bore Jacob many sons, one after another, and Rachel became pained.

She turned to God and cried day and night, pleading with Him to open her womb, to bless her as He had blessed her sister. God remembered her. Genesis 30:22 says:

"Then God remembered Rachel; he listened to her and enabled her to conceive.

> *"She gave birth to her first son and named him Joseph, saying, "May the Lord add to me another son" (Genesis 30:24)*

And God granted her heart's desire in Genesis 35:16-17! She bore another son for Jacob and named him Benoni because he was born with hard labor, but Jacob changed his name to Benjamin.

Rachel's faith in God was evident in her waiting on Him for a child for over 20 years. She believed God would give her children, so she never stopped praying and crying to Him. Even when God blessed her with her first son, she named Joseph, which means 'God will give.' She was blessed with another before tragedy struck.

Parallels Between These Women's Struggles and Modern-Day Challenges Women Face Today.

The stories of the women of Genesis resonate with many challenges women face today. Here are parallels between these women's struggles and modern-day challenges:

Rachel and Sarah's deep longing for children mirrors the emotional and psychological challenges many women face today when dealing with infertility or delays in starting a family. Their struggle with jealousy was real. Many women today experience the pain of infertility or delays in conceiving, especially when they feel pressured by society to start a family.

Like Eve, many women today face choices that might have nasty consequences, such as career changes, relationships, and parenting decisions. The burden of these decisions can lead to guilt, regret, or loss. After making life-altering decisions, many women desire redemption, forgiveness, and a fresh start, striving to rebuild and renew their lives through growth, faith, or support systems.

Hagar became a single mother. Many women are familiar with this these days. Her story reflects the struggles of many single mothers today who face social stigma and the challenges of raising children without a partner. However, she was resilient, and as a true survivor, she raised her son to be strong and mighty in the wilderness.

Like the story of the two sisters, Rachel and Leah, many modern women get caught in a cycle of comparison and competition. Whether in careers, relationships, motherhood, or physical appearance, women today are often pressured to measure up to others. Social media doesn't help matters. Most women feel inadequate and envious of others when they see the love others get from their fans and followers. This competition is why there are not many genuine relationships between women.

Lessons to Learn from the Women of Genesis

These biblical stories offer timeless lessons that are relevant today. Here are lessons drawn from these Bible stories:

- Like Rachel and Sarah, continue to pray and trust God's timing, even when life doesn't unfold as expected. Hold onto God's promises and remain faithful, even when faced with doubt and delays.

- Learn from Eve that while mistakes have consequences, God's forgiveness and redemption are always available to those who seek it.

- Like Leah, instead of being bitter, she focused on God. He can turn you into wonder and give you a legacy that lasts for generations. Isaiah 60:22 says, *"The least of you will become a thousand, the smallest a mighty nation. I am the Lord; in its time I will do this swiftly."*

- As Hagar acknowledged, remember that God sees you in your struggles and will provide for your needs, even when you feel unseen. He is faithful.

Journaling Prompt

Create a personal faith journal entry reflecting on a time when your faith got tested. Write about how you can draw inspiration from the women of Genesis to strengthen your faith in similar situations.

Chapter 3: Courageous Leaders in Exodus

The Bible has many stories of women who displayed courage despite adversities. Some are known, while most are not. Like the silent characters in the background who get things done, these women actively serve in their capacity. Some were even more courageous than men, contributing to fulfilling God's plan for the Israelites.

The book of Exodus captures the stories of these women. They include Jochebed, Miriam, Shiphrah, Puah, and Pharaoh's daughter. This chapter explores the lives of these courageous women and how they defied the norms, took risks, and significantly impacted the course of events.

The book of Exodus captures the stories of these women.'

You might read about these names for the first time, but rest assured, their stories will inspire you. By the end of this chapter, you will have experienced the strength and determination of the women of Exodus. Are you ready to discover how powerful you are as a woman when you choose to be brave? Find a quiet place. It's time to study.

Jochebed | The Prophetic Womb (Exodus 2)

Her name may not be as popular as her children's, but no one would know of the prophet Moses and the priest Aaron if it wasn't for her sacrifice and courage. Jochebed was a woman of great courage and strong faith. She was a Levite and married Amram (Exodus 2:1).

They got married in the land of Egypt during the reign of a new Pharaoh, who knew nothing about Joseph and how he helped Egypt become a place of abundance. This new Pharaoh saw how the children of Israel were multiplying and sought to turn them into slaves because he was afraid of them.

His fear caused him to pass a decree that all newly born male children by Hebrew women be killed. Unfortunately, Jochebed was also a Hebrew woman and became pregnant during this period. When she gave birth and saw that the baby was a boy, she was sorely afraid.

Looking at the child, she realized he was no ordinary child. So, she did the unthinkable. She could tell God had a plan for her son's life, so she chose faith over fear. She hid the baby from Pharaoh and his minions for as long as possible. She succeeded for three months. She carefully moved him around, fed him, and protected him with wisdom, knowing the consequences of her actions if caught. God watched over her and her son.

After the third month, Jochebed realized she could no longer hide him. So, she crafted a sturdy basket, and with faith that could move mountains, she placed her baby boy inside the basket and on the river Nile. She carefully used materials that would keep the basket afloat. After praying to God to keep her child safe, she turned and walked away. Matthew 19:26:

> *"Jesus looked at them and said, "With man, this is impossible, but with God all things are possible."*

As God would have it, the baby floated to the side of the river into the brushes, where the Pharoah's daughter came to have her bath. The princess saw the floating basket and opened it. The baby cried, and she felt pity for him. As she carried the child, she was at a loss for what to do with it until a little girl ran to her and offered to help her find a nurse.

Unbeknownst to the princess, the little girl was the baby's big sister, and the nurse she found was the baby's mother. Jochebed couldn't contain her joy at being reunited with her son under the watchful eye of the princess. She finally had the chance to nurse the baby without fear of being killed by Pharaoh. She never exposed herself to the princess. She was known as the baby's nurse and had no problems with the title.

Raising the boy, Jochebed taught him the ways of the Lord. She let him know he was an Israelite, not an Egyptian, even though he was groomed and treated like an Egyptian prince. The baby grew into a fine young man in the Egyptian palace, but his heart was with his people as his mother taught him.

This baby was the prophet Moses. The same Moses God used to lead the Israelites out of slavery and bondage in the land of Egypt, where they had suffered for over 430 years. Jochebed's courage and unshakable faith in God to make a way where they seemed to be none made her the mother of influential figures in the Bible, Miriam, Moses, and Aaron, who grew up to be prophets.

Her faith and courage are why the Israelites tasted freedom after so many centuries. Jochebed is a testament to how one woman can impact generations by being brave, courageous, and having faith in God.

Miriam | The Prophetess (Exodus 2)

Jochebed's firstborn, Miriam, is another influential figure in the Bible that many don't know about. Her role in the deliverance of Israel is often overlooked. She was born during a dangerous time in Egypt when Pharaoh decreed all the Hebrew male infants be killed.

God, in his infinite wisdom, caused her to be born a girl so she could play her role without being noticed or affected by the decree passed over the land. When her baby brother, Moses, was born, their mother, Jochebed, hid him for three months. Miriam did all she could to help her mom protect Moses. She looked after him when their mom couldn't.

She was the one who warned her mom when officers or soldiers were approaching so she could quickly hide the baby. As a little girl, Miriam was efficient as the protective big sister. Like her mother, Miriam had faith that Moses would grow and become a great man. Determined to keep the child safe, Miriam would protect him with her life.

When their mother set baby Moses in a basket and placed him on the river Nile, Miriam's eyes shone with unshed tears but steeled her heart and trusted God as her mother had taught her. After her mother had left the river, Miriam remained close to the river bank, watching her baby brother like his guardian angel float on the river.

Alert and attentive, she followed the basket's movement with remarkable bravery and maturity unusual for someone her age. She watched as the princess and her maidens came to the river and hid while keeping an eye on the floating basket. To her greatest surprise, the basket floated to the princess. The princess took her brother out of the river and the basket.

Miriam boldly approached the princess and sweetly offered to help her find a Hebrew woman to nurse the baby. Pharaoh's daughter agreed without hesitation. Miriam quickly ran to tell her mother about God's miracle. The young girl reappeared at the river bank with her mother and a bright smile on her face. She was so excited (Exodus 2:4-9). This act saved Moses' life and allowed Jochebed to care for her son during his early years. She used this time to instill in Moses the faith and identity of his Hebrew heritage.

By the time she reached adulthood, Miriam was a prophetess alongside her brothers Moses and Aaron, who also became a prophet and a priest. After the Israelites' dramatic escape from Egypt, when God parted the Red Sea, allowing them to cross safely, and then drowned the pursuing Egyptian army, Miriam led the women of Israel in a song of victory. She took a tambourine in her hand, and all the women followed her with tambourines and dancing. Miriam sang:

> *"Sing to the LORD, for he has triumphed gloriously; the horse and his rider he has thrown into the sea"* (Exodus 15:20-21)

And this pleased the Lord.

As an adult, Miriam's role among the Israelites became more prominent. She is referred to as a prophetess, indicating her spiritual significance and leadership among her people (Exodus 15:20). This moment demonstrated her leadership and her deep faith in God. She played a vital role in encouraging and uplifting the people's spirits through worship and praise, celebrating God's deliverance and mighty acts.

Like every human, Miriam wasn't perfect. Once, she spoke against Moses, saying:

> "Has the LORD indeed spoken only through Moses? Has he not spoken through us also?" (Numbers 12:2)

God heard this and was displeased with their challenge to Moses' authority.

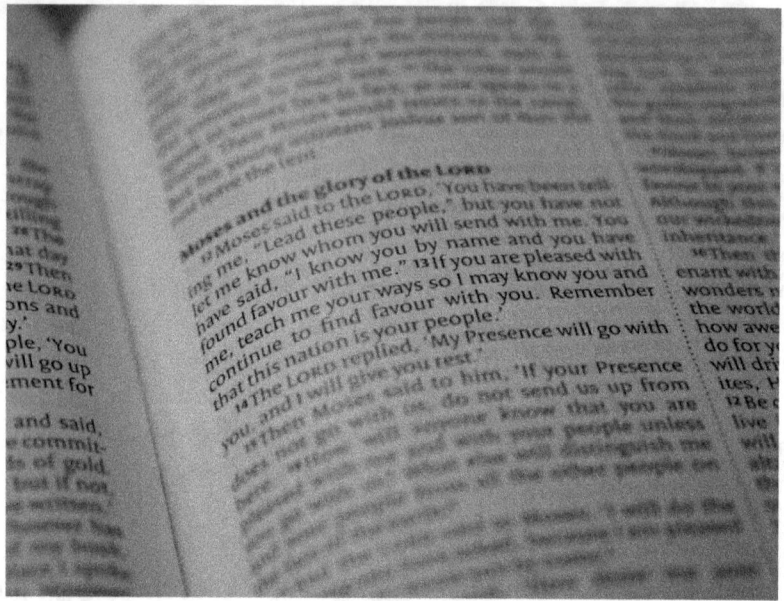

Miriam spoke against Moses, but God defended him, for he directly spoke to him.'

God called Moses, Aaron, and Miriam to the Tent of Meeting and descended in a pillar of cloud. God defended Moses, saying he was unlike any prophet because He spoke to Moses "face to face" (Numbers 12:8). As a punishment for her actions, Miriam was struck with leprosy, her skin becoming "white as snow" (Numbers 12:10). Moses interceded for Miriam and God instructed that she be confined outside their camp for seven days after which He would heal her. She obeyed and was healed. It was a humbling lesson for Miriam, and despite her moment of weakness, she remained a respected leader among the Israelites.

Shiphrah and Puah | The Courageous Midwives (Exodus 1)

During Pharaoh's decree to kill all male infants born by Hebrew women, God strategically placed two Hebrew midwives in Egypt to save some children. Shiphrah and Paul stood up to one of the most powerful rulers in the world out of fear of God and little respect for their lives.

Pharaoh feared the Israelites would become too powerful and join Egypt's enemies whenever war broke out. He forced the Israelites into harsh labor and oppressed them. However, instead of reducing, the number of Israelites grew. They multiplied and spread further across Egypt.

Realizing his plan failed, Pharaoh tried another strategy. He got into the business of shedding innocent blood – the blood of young infant males. He aimed to control Israel's population to ensure they never became as mighty as the Egyptians. For his plan to work, he summoned the midwives who tended to the Hebrew women because he couldn't appear the instant a child was born to kill the males.

As God would have it, the midwives in charge were Shiphrah and Puah – women who feared God. Pharaoh gave them a direct command that put the women in a dangerous and difficult position. If they obeyed Pharaoh, they would go against their conscience and God's will. However, they would face severe punishment, even death, if disobeyed. Their fear of God won the battle because, as Proverbs 29:25 says:

"Fear of man will prove to be a snare, but whoever trusts in the Lord is kept safe."

They knew that life is sacred, and God gives life and has the right to take it. So, they disobeyed Pharaoh's order. They risked their lives and freedom to let the male babies live instead of killing them. It was a brave and risky decision. They had faith and courage to stand up to powerful authority, knowing that what they did was right before God, even if dangerous.

When Pharaoh learned that the number of babies born was increasing instead of decreasing, he called the women to his palace and questioned them. The women answered him with wisdom, explaining that the wives had already delivered the babies by the time they arrived at a Hebrew house. There was nothing they could do about it. Pharaoh believed them.

God was pleased with Shiphrah and Puah for their fear of Him and their courage to do what was right. God blessed them because they feared Him and chose to preserve life. The Bible says that God dealt well with the midwives, and because they feared Him, He gave them families of their own:

"So God was kind to the midwives and the people increased and became even more numerous. And because the midwives feared God, he gave them families of their own..."
(Exodus 1:20–21)

God sees peoples' hearts and blesses those who stand for the truth, even when the odds are against them.

Pharaoh's Daughter | Moses's Foster Mom
(Exodus 2)

Did you know that Moses' biological mother did not name him? Indeed not. Even though he reunited with his mom after the Nile River drama, she never named him because he was not her son – at least to the rest of Egypt and for the sake of both their lives.

Pharaoh's daughter named Moses in Exodus 2:10:

> *"When the child grew older, she took him to Pharaoh's daughter, and he became her son. She named him Moses, saying, "I drew him out of the water."*

From the moment Pharaoh's daughter laid her eyes on the little crying mess that floated in a basket on the river, she felt responsible for the child.

Interestingly, she knew the boy was Hebrew. She also knew the decree her father, the Pharaoh, had passed concerning them:

> *"She opened it and saw the baby. He was crying, and she felt sorry for him. "This is one of the Hebrew babies," she said."*
> (Exodus 2:6)

However, the princess was not heartless like her father.

Pharaoh's daughter took the crying boy from the basket and consoled him. She felt much compassion for the baby. While she tended to the child, cooing and rocking him back and forth, a little girl ran up to her. Her maidens tried to stop the girl, but Pharaoh's daughter told them to let her through. The girl told the princess she knew someone who would take good care of the baby. It was painfully obvious the princess had no idea what to do with the baby as it wailed.

Pharaoh's daughter consented, and the little girl disappeared only to reappear with a middle-aged, pleasant-looking woman. The princess watched with wide eyes how the baby immediately became quiet the moment the woman took him from her arms. 'This little girl is a godsend,' she thought.

She told the woman to take the child with her and nurse him, offering to pay the woman wages for caring for the boy. The woman happily agreed. Exodus 2:9:

> *"Pharaoh's daughter said to her, "Take this baby and nurse him for me, and I will pay you." So, the woman took the baby and nursed him."*

When the child grew, his mother (the nurse) returned him to Pharaoh's daughter. She was pleased with how much he had grown. The princess took the boy and named him Moses. From that moment onward, he became her son and was raised as a prince in Pharaoh's palace.

Rescuing a Hebrew child was risky, probably one of the riskiest things Pharaoh's daughter had ever done. But she did it, anyway. Her kindness and compassion fueled her courage to keep the boy under Pharaoh's roof. Her fear of her father and his decree were less important than her humanity. She was determined to do what was right. Pharaoh's daughter unknowingly aligned with God's purpose and made a name for herself as a great woman in the Bible.

Rescuing a Hebrew child was risky, probably one of the riskiest things Pharaoh's daughter had ever done.'

The story of Moses and the deliverance of Israel cannot be recounted without mentioning the kind and courageous princess. She could have easily turned a blind eye to the floating basket or had the baby presented to her father when she saw he was Hebrew. Hence, a divine Pharaoh's daughter became an influential figure in Israel's history intervention. She understood God's purpose for this child and was ready to play her part in it, even if it went against her people.

Lessons to Learn from the Courageous Women of Exodus

You can learn many lessons from Jochebed, Miriam, Shiphrah, Puah, and Pharaoh's daughter. These women acted bravely under challenging situations and wrote their names in the sands of time. They became icons, women known for their courage, faith in God, and compassion for humanity.

You can see a good display of the power of a mother's love and faith in the story of Jochebed. Despite the fear and danger that clouded the land, Jochebed chose to protect her son. She hid Moses for three months, bravely keeping him safe even though she knew she would be severely punished if caught.

She displayed more of her brave side as she set the baby on the river because she did not know what would happen to him. From Jochebed's story, you learn that courage is trusting in a plan greater than yours, even when the future is uncertain, not just jumping headfirst into a situation. Her faith in God's plan for her son gave her the strength to let him go. Would you have done the same if you were in her shoes?

The courageous big sister, Miriam, took responsibility at a young age. As she watched the basket float away from her mother on its own accord, she couldn't do much to help her brother, but she stayed. She couldn't swim to the baby if the basket suddenly got punctured and sank. She watched him go regardless.

The little girl knew something the adults didn't, and she was there for it. She wanted to ensure nothing happened to her baby brother. Miriam quickly seized the opportunity when Pharaoh's daughter found the basket and saw Moses inside. Sometimes, opportunities can be spotted from a mile away if people are as discerning as Miriam. They can make the most of it as God would have wanted. Miriam painted a clear picture in her story: courage is not about age or size; it is willing to step up and help when things don't go as smoothly as expected. It means being watchful, wise, and ready to act, even when scared or unsure.

The two Hebrew midwives feared the Pharaoh, but their fear of God was greater. Are you a person who fears God? Will you willingly go against laws if they do not align with God's will? It's usually easier said than done, but Shiphrah and Puah proved that with their courage, it was doable. They blatantly disobeyed the Pharaoh and used their wisdom to evade punishment. Their actions could have cost them everything, but they put God first.

Matthew 6:33 says:

> *"But seek first his kingdom and his righteousness, and all these things will be given to you as well." God let those baby boys live and gave them families. John 12:25 says, "Anyone who loves their life will lose it, while anyone who hates their life in this world will keep it for eternal life."*

These women loved not their lives. Instead, they dedicated their lives to ensuring the Hebrew children were born and grew mighty no matter the cost.

What about Pharaoh's daughter? She was the daughter of the man who ordered the killings of the babies, yet she was unafraid to keep one under his roof. She took Moses into her home and raised him as her son, even though she knew it went against her father's rule.

Courage means following your heart and being kind, even when it goes against what people expect from you, like Pharaoh's daughter, so long as it is right in God's eyes. Being kind can lead to brave decisions, and compassion is strength.

Courage comes in many forms. You can see how it is beautifully displayed in these women's lives. It can be shown through faith, responsibility, doing what is right, or being compassionate.

Journaling Prompt

Write a letter to one of the women in Exodus that inspires you. Tell her about your struggles and how her story of bravery and resilience helped you.

Chapter 4: Ruth and Esther: Lessons in Love and Compassion

Love and compassion are two vital tenets of a good Christian. Indeed, a good person. Apostle Paul, speaking on love, wrote an entire chapter to remind believers of the importance of love.

Love and compassion are two vital tenets of a good Christian.[10]

1 Corinthians 13:1-13:

"If I speak in the tongues of men or of angels, but do not have love, I am only a resounding gong or a clanging cymbal. If I have the gift of prophecy and can fathom all mysteries and all knowledge, and if I have a faith that can move mountains, but do not have love, I am nothing. If I give all I possess to the poor and give over my body to hardship that I may boast, but do not have love, I gain nothing. Love is patient, love is kind. It does not envy, it does not boast, it is not proud. It does not dishonor others, it is not self-seeking, it is not easily angered, it keeps no record of wrongs. Love does not delight in evil but rejoices with the truth. It always protects, always trusts, always hopes, always perseveres. Love never fails. But where there are prophecies, they will cease; where there are tongues, they will be stilled; where there is knowledge, it will pass away. For we know in part, and we prophesy in part, but when completeness comes, what is in part disappears. When I was a child, I talked like a child, I thought like a child, I reasoned like a child. When I became a man, I put the ways of childhood behind me. For now, we see only a reflection as in a mirror; then we shall see face to face. Now I know in part; then I shall know fully, even as I am fully known. And now these three remain: faith, hope, and love. But the greatest of these is love."

Now, if your love looks nothing like the love described above, you have some work to do. Lucky for you, this chapter will guide you when you are confused about what love should look like.

Jesus taught about love during His time on earth. In John 13:34, he said:

"A new command I give you: Love one another. As I have loved you, so you must love one another."

Matthew 22:34-40:

"Hearing that Jesus had silenced the Sadducees, the Pharisees got together. One of them, an expert in the law, tested him with this question: "Teacher, which is the greatest commandment in the Law?" Jesus replied: "Love the Lord your God with all your heart and with all your soul and with all your mind. This is the first and greatest commandment.

And the second is like it: Love your neighbor as yourself. All the Law and the Prophets hang on these two commandments."

This chapter is about love, love, and more love. Right next to the theme of love is compassion. God is a loving and compassionate father. Micah 7:18 says:

"Who is a God like you, who pardons sin and forgives the transgression of the remnant of his inheritance? You do not stay angry forever but delight to show mercy." In John 3:16, the Bible states, "For God so loved the world that he gave his one and only Son, that whoever believes in him shall not perish but have eternal life."

God is love. John the Beloved confirms this in 1 John 4:7-12:

"Dear friends, let us love one another, for love comes from God. Everyone who loves has been born of God and knows God. Whoever does not love does not know God because God is love. This is how God showed his love among us: He sent his one and only Son into the world that we might live through him. This is love: not that we loved God, but that he loved us and sent his Son as an atoning sacrifice for our sins. Dear friends, since God so loved us, we also ought to love one another. No one has ever seen God, but if we love one another, God lives in us, and his love is made complete in us."

Many characters in the Bible showcase love and compassion. This chapter focuses on two spectacular women in the Old Testament, Ruth and Esther. They had love and compassion embedded in their stories. These women displayed remarkable selflessness, compassion, loyalty, courage, and, most importantly, love.

The Story of Ruth

For a time in Israel, the people did not have a king. Instead, God raised leaders, "judges," to guide the people; this era was known as the "era of judges." The book lies between the book of Ruth and the book of Joshua.

When Joshua died, there was no one to rule or lead the people like Moses had, giving rise to the need for judges in the land. However, the people of Israel had a problem. They were fundamentally stubborn and disobedient. Sometimes, they worshipped other gods or did things entirely against God's commands.

They went against the covenant God made with Abraham so many times with their tendency to idolize manmade gods.

"I will establish my covenant as an everlasting covenant between me and you and your descendants after you for the generations to come, to be your God and the God of your descendants after you" (Genesis 17:7)

Due to their behavior, God allowed difficult situations, like famine or enemy attacks, as punishment. The people cried out to God when the suffering became too much. He showed mercy by raising another judge to save them. It was a never-ending cycle with Israel.

There was a famine during this time in the small town of Bethlehem. Yes. The same Bethlehem where Jesus was born. People were suffering from the drought and crops were dying, which meant no food for the masses. A man named Elimelek from Bethlehem took his family to Moab, a nearby country, because of the famine. He ran away from the land God gave his people because the suffering was too much.

Elimelek took his wife, Naomi, and their two sons with him. It was a difficult decision to leave since Moab and Israel were not on friendly terms, and often the tension brewed between them. However, Elimelek believed that going to a place where they could find food, even if it were an enemy land, would be better.

Unfortunately for the small family, tragedy struck. Elimelek died not long after they arrived in Moab. His sons, who took wives from the Moabites, died 10 years later, leaving Elimelek's wife, Naomi, and his sons' wives, Ruth and Orpah, widows. After burning her husband and sons, Naomi heard that God had remembered Bethlehem, and the famine was over. So, she prepared to return to her homeland.

Naomi called her daughters-in-law and advised them to go to their mother's houses and find new husbands since they were still young. It was an emotional day for the women. They wept bitterly. The young women told their mother-in-law they would willingly go with her wherever she went.

Naomi tried to convince them:

"But Naomi said, "Return home, my daughters. Why would you come with me? Am I going to have any more sons, who could become your husbands? Return home, my daughters; I am too old to have another husband. Even if I thought there was still hope for me—even if I had a husband tonight and

then gave birth to sons— would you wait until they grew up? Would you remain unmarried for them? No, my daughters. It is more bitter for me than for you, because the LORD's hand has turned against me!" (Ruth 1:11-13)

Ruth was committed to caring for her late husband's mother.[11]

Orpah saw sense in Naomi's words and returned to her mother's house. She kissed Naomi, packed up her belongings, and left. On the other hand, Ruth wasn't willing to let go of her mother-in-law. Naomi looked at her and said, *"Look, said Naomi, your sister-in-law is going back to her people and her gods. Go back with her."* But Ruth didn't budge.

She told Naomi in Ruth 1:16-17:

"Don't urge me to leave you or to turn back from you. Where you go I will go, and where you stay I will stay. Your people will be my people and your God my God. Where you die I will die, and there I will be buried. May the Lord deal with me, be it ever so severely, if even death separates you and me."

Naomi realized Ruth was determined to travel with her. She was deeply touched. She stopped urging Ruth to leave, and they returned to Bethlehem together.

Ruth was committed to caring for her late husband's mother. The woman was already old and could do very little for herself. She made a vow to follow Naomi to the ends of the earth, and she meant it.

While they were in Bethlehem, Ruth went to the fields to gather leftover grain for her and her mother-in-law. With Naomi's blessing, she set out and found herself in a field belonging to one of late Elimelek's distant relatives. The field owner, Boaz, came to greet the harvesters, and Ruth caught his eye. She wasn't a familiar face but had a beautiful face, and Boaz couldn't help but ask the overseer of his harvesters about her.

The overseer explained how Ruth came to the field and humbly asked to pick up the leftover grains as the harvesters did their job. She worked tirelessly. The overseer told him about her kindness toward her mother-in-law, whom she followed from Moab into a foreign land.

After hearing about Ruth's story, Boaz called Ruth and told her she could work in his field permanently. He commanded the men in his field not to touch her and provided everything she needed to be comfortable in his field. Ruth was surprised at his kindness toward her when he barely knew her. Boaz smiled and told her he had heard her troubles and her kindness to Naomi and assured her she would be safe with him (Ruth 2:8-11).

Boaz called her to eat with the harvesters at dinner time and offered her food. She ate until satisfied and even had some to take home to Naomi. When she left the field, Boaz ensured Ruth had more than enough grain to take home for her and Naomi.

Ruth 2:15-18:

> *"As she got up to glean, Boaz gave orders to his men, "Let her gather among the sheaves and don't reprimand her. Even pull out some stalks for her from the bundles and leave them for her to pick up, and don't rebuke her." So, Ruth gleaned in the field until evening. Then she threshed the barley she had gathered, and it amounted to about an ephah. She carried it back to town, and her mother-in-law saw how much she had gathered. Ruth also brought out and gave her what she had left over after she had eaten enough."*

Back home, Naomi couldn't believe her eyes when she saw Ruth. The younger woman told her all that transpired between her and Boaz at the field. Naomi advised her to continue working in his field because he was obviously fond of her.

After learning that Boaz was a relative who could redeem their property, Naomi devised a plan. Following Naomi's guidance, Ruth approached Boaz on the threshing floor, humbly asking him to spread his cloak over her as a symbol of protection and redemption. Boaz, moved by her request, agreed, but there was a closer relative who had the first right to redeem. Not wanting to miss his chance, Boaz quickly went to the town gate the next day to present his case- Boaz was freed to act as the kinsman-redeemer for Naomi and Ruth.

Boaz declared his intention to redeem Naomi's land and marry Ruth. The elders and people blessed the union, saying:

> *"May the Lord make the woman who is coming into your home like Rachel and Leah, who together built up the house of Israel"* (Ruth 4:11).

Boaz and Ruth married, and God blessed them with a son, Obed. Once filled with bitterness and despair, Naomi held her grandson in her arms – her joy and hope restored. The town's women celebrated with her, saying:

> *"Praise be to the Lord, who this day has not left you without a guardian-redeemer. May he become famous throughout Israel! He will renew your life and sustain you in your old age. For your daughter-in-law, who loves you and who is better to you than seven sons, has given him birth."* (Ruth 4:14-15)

Obed would become the grandfather of King David, linking Ruth, a Moabite woman, into the lineage of Israel's greatest King and Savior of the world, Jesus Christ.

The Story of Queen Esther

At one time in history, Jewish people lived under Persian rule, exiled from their homeland. King Xerxes, who knew nothing about the Jewish people, ruled the Persian Empire. The Israelites weren't numerous and surrounded by people who didn't understand or respect their faith.

Although they lived and worked in the empire, they always risked persecution. A high-ranking official in King Xerxes' court, Haman, developed a hatred for the Jewish people, causing them to live in fear.

Haman's hatred was personal. He encountered Mordecai at the gate, a Jew who refused to bow to him. In his anger, Haman plotted to destroy all the Jews in the empire, convincing King Xerxes to issue a decree to have them killed (Esther 3:8-11).

While the feud between Haman and Mordecai lurked. A different drama was unfolding in the palace. King Xerxes dismissed his wife, Queen Vashti, because of her attitude, creating a vacuum in the palace and a need for a new queen. The King's servants suggested he permit them to search the kingdom for young virgins to select a new queen. The King gave his word, and the search began.

Mordecai was the orphaned Jewish girl Esther's uncle. As soon as he heard of the King's request, he recruited Esther. She was very beautiful, and Mordecai had no doubt she would be selected.

When presented to the King, Esther found favor in his sight, and he selected her to be his new queen.[13]

When Esther made it to the palace for selection, she found favor with Hegai, the keeper of the women. He gave her special oils and quickly gave her what she needed to win the King's heart. When presented to the King, Esther found favor in his sight, and he selected her to be his new queen. Esther's status was changed overnight – from the orphaned Jewish girl to the new queen of the Persian Empire. (Esther 2:7-17). Esther's rise to queen was part of a divine plan. Mordecai, who had cared for Esther, instructed her not to reveal her Jewish identity (Esther 2:10).

Once, Mordecai overheard people discussing the assassination of the King and told Esther. She quickly informed the King. He immediately investigated and learned that, indeed, plans to assassinate him were afoot. King Xerxes had the suspects hanged, and Mordecai's name was written in the King's book of Chronicles (Esther 2:21-23).

Esther had become queen, so Mordecai discussed the problem of the Jews with her, particularly Haman's role. When Mordecai learned of Haman's plan to destroy the Jews, he tore his clothes and put on sackcloth and ashes, mourning for his people (Esther 4:1).

He sent word to Esther, urging her to go to the king and beg for mercy on behalf of her people. It seemed a simple request. However, in Persian law, anyone who approached the king without being summoned could be put to death unless the king extended his golden scepter to them (Esther 4:11).

Esther was determined to deliver her people despite the possible consequences of her actions. She asked Mordecai and all the Jews in Susa too fast for three days and nights on her behalf, saying, *"I will go to the king, even though it is against the law. And if I perish, I perish"* (Esther 4:16). The young Queen would willingly lay down her life for her people. She trusted that God would be with her when she went before the King.

After fasting and praying, she went to the king. Like someone spellbound, the moment the King laid his eyes on her, he extended his golden scepter, sparing her life (Esther 5:1-2). Instead of immediately pleading for her people, she applied wisdom. Esther invited King Xerxes and Haman to a banquet she had prepared. At the banquet, her husband asked her to demand anything, and it would be granted. She only requested they attend another banquet (Esther 5:4-8).

This delay was a strategic move. Esther was wise to wait for the right moment to reveal Haman's plot. That night, the king could not sleep and ordered the Book of Chronicles to be read to him. He learned of Mordecai's earlier act of saving his life and realized Mordecai had not received a rewarded (Esther 6:1-3). The King called for Haman and had him honor Mordecai, the man he despised, by leading him through the city on the king's horse, saying, *"This is what is done for the man the king delights to honor!"* (Esther 6:6-11).

At the second banquet, Esther revealed her Jewish identity and exposed Haman's wicked plan to cut off her people from the land. Turning to her husband, she said:

"If I have found favor with you, Your Majesty, and if it pleases you, grant me my life—this is my petition. And spare my people—this is my request. For I and my people have been sold to be destroyed, killed, and annihilated. If we had merely been sold as male and female slaves, I would have kept quiet, because no such distress would justify disturbing the king." (Esther 7:3-4)

King Xerxes was shocked and enraged that anyone would dare do such a thing. He asked Esther who the unfortunate soul was, and she pointed to Haman (Esther 7:5-6).

Esther and Mordecai were part of God's larger plan to protect and deliver the Jewish people from destruction. After Esther revealed Haman's plot, King Xerxes ordered Haman to hang from the gallows he had prepared for Mordecai (Esther 7:9-10). The king issued a new decree allowing the Jews to defend themselves against their enemies (Esther 8:11). On the day the enemies had hoped to overpower the Jews, the tables had turned. The Jews gained the upper hand over those who hated them (Esther 9:1).

As the issue with Haman died down, Esther's uncle, Mordecai, was elevated to a position of high honor, and the Jewish people were saved from their enemies. They celebrated the festival of Purim to celebrate their deliverance (Esther 9:20-22).

Lessons for Today

Ruth's vow to Naomi proved her deep love and compassion for her mother-in-law. She was willing to leave everything behind to support Naomi in her time of need, which was an incredibly selfless act. Like Ruth, Esther was also selfless. She risked her life to save her people from destruction. Her love for her people was greater than her fear of death. True love is sacrificial and more than mere words. You must act it out. Don't worry. It will be easy if your feelings are genuine. You should be willing to put the needs of others before yours.

Ruth, as a Moabite widow, had every right to return to her people and start a new life after her husband's death. Yet, she chose to travel with Naomi to a land she knew nothing about and live among people she had never seen. Ruth was indeed a woman of faith. Esther said, *"If I perish, I perish..."* with a heart determined to deliver her people. She was a woman of great faith. Faith in God is the fastest way to gain victory over a situation. 1 John 5:14 says, *"For everyone born of God overcomes the world. This is the victory that has overcome the world, even our faith."*

Ruth and Esther were empaths. Their compassion for others led to their upliftment. As an empath, you don't only feel for others. You act on their behalf.

A leader is not a loud and obnoxious person in a group. No. A leader is someone with quiet strength, good intentions, strategic thinking skills, courageous, and wise. Ruth and Esther were leaders who conquered all with love and compassion.

Journaling Prompt

Create a journal entry listing acts of kindness for the next three days. Aim to commit to these, journal daily, and track how you feel.

Chapter 5: Spiritual Lessons from the Psalms

What comes to your mind when you hear the word Psalms? A song? King David? If you thought of these, you have a good idea of what a psalm is about. However, a psalm could be a hymn, a poem, a prayer, or a song.

The book of Psalms comprises many songs and prayers encouraging people to praise God.[18]

Many songwriters today get inspiration for songs from the book of Psalms. Yes. There is a whole book filled with Psalms. Most chapters in the book were written by a man after God's own heart, King David. Many secrets were shared, mysteries unveiled, and prophecies told. The book of Psalms is highly spiritual. In Colossian 3:16, Paul speaks to the believers:

> *"Let the message of Christ dwell among you richly as you teach and admonish one another with all wisdom through psalms, hymns, and songs from the Spirit, singing to God with gratitude in your hearts."*

Are you looking for words of wisdom? You won't be disappointed. Are you looking for instructions? The Psalms have plenty. Are you looking for unique songs to praise and worship God? Just sit with the book of Psalms.

The book of Psalms comprises many songs and prayers encouraging people to praise God. It speaks of God's greatness and the wonderful things He has done. Psalms tells of God's faithfulness, especially during challenging times. The book reminds God's people that His Word should be at the center of their lives.

This chapter breaks from studying Biblical characters and explores the rich spiritual insights in the book of Psalms. Insights that will guide you to build a strong and resilient spiritual foundation.

The Book of Psalms is one of the most cherished books of the Bible. It often gets referred to as the "heart of the Bible." The book is a collection of songs, prayers, and hymns written by several authors anointed by God. You probably didn't know this before – one of the most popular writers is King David. Other writers include Moses and Asaph, the descendants of Korah, King Solomon, and Ethan and Heman, the Ezrahites.

This chapter aims to inspire women to deepen their relationship with God through the wisdom, prayer, and praise encapsulated in the Psalms. As you read, you will find practical ways to apply the Psalms' teachings to your daily life for spiritual growth and strength.

The Significance of the Psalms

Throughout Psalms, there is a clear picture of how God lovingly guides His people, always showing them the right path. The writers of these songs were always ready to praise and worship God. Every page in the book of Psalms is laced with strong love and devotion to God, and there are many moments in which they express their deep trust and joy in Him.

Initially titled Tehillim, which means "praise songs" in Hebrew, the book expresses a wide range of human emotions and spiritual experiences. It is composed of 150 psalms. King David is credited with writing many of them. The Psalms hold a special place in the hearts of believers. People across cultures and ages have learned to effectively speak the language of prayer and worship through their fellowship with the book of Psalms. It has proven a source of comfort, guidance, and strength for people seeking a closer relationship with God.

Every aspect of human life, from joy and praise to despair and repentance, makes them deeply relevant to personal spiritual development. As Psalm 119:105 says, "Your word is a lamp to my feet and a light to my path." The Psalms offer insight and direction to help believers navigate this tricky thing called life and the challenges within, and they present an opportunity for spiritual growth.

Key Themes in the Psalms

Trusting in God

One prominent theme in the book of Psalms is trust in God. Finding more peace in life, reducing stress, especially as a woman, and completely trusting God are the most important things you can do. Trusting people can be difficult because they often disappoint. Psalms 146:3 says, *"Do not put your trust in princes, in human beings, who cannot save."*

The world is full of uncertainties and challenges, so it is difficult to rely on it for comfort or security. However, with God, it's like lying in your mother's pouch like a baby kangaroo. You are shielded and kept safe. Throughout the Bible, God repeatedly asks believers to put their trust in Him alone. Fun fact: It was not only a suggestion. This command comes from God's deep desire for your well-being. He wants to ensure you're doing great.

Trusting God is a wise decision. You feel much closer to Him, giving you the strength to face whatever comes your way. Doubts are normal, but your new normal can be knowing that God understands your nature, your struggle with fear and worry about the future, and trusting Him instead.

There is a recurring message throughout the Psalms - whenever you feel overwhelmed by stress, remember to turn to God and trust in His plan for you. His unchanging nature and steadfast love make Him the most trustworthy. Psalm 56:3-4 says, "*When I am afraid, I put my trust in you. In God, whose word I praise—in God I trust and am not afraid. What can mere mortals do to me?*" The more you read His Word, especially the Psalms, you will find comfort in knowing God is always with you, guiding and loving you unconditionally.

For study purposes, here are 10 Psalms proving you can trust God entirely. You can read them whenever you feel your faith is wavering.

- Psalm 11
- Psalm 16
- Psalm 23
- Psalm 27
- Psalm 62
- Psalm 63
- Psalm 91
- Psalm 121
- Psalm 125
- Psalm 131

Worship

Many praise and adoration expressions for God speak of His greatness, mercy, and power in the Psalms. It contains poems and prayers promoting the worship of God in every circumstance, whether overjoyed or weighed down by sorrow. Worship is about opening your heart to God and recognizing His majesty and glory.

The Bible often refers to God as a shepherd caring for His sheep. In worship, you recognize your place before God: the sheep of His pasture. Psalm 100:3 says, "*Know that the Lord is God. It is he who made us, and we are his; we are his people, the sheep of his pasture.*"

The Bible often refers to God as a shepherd caring for His sheep.[14]

You are His creation. Being dependent on His love and provision is not a crime. It is how He expects you to live. As a child of God, you cannot fully exist outside Him. Acts 17:28:

"For in him we live and move and have our being. As some of your own poets have said, We are his offspring."

The act of worship in the Psalms is deeply personal. The Psalms urges you to come before God with an open heart, offering Him praises and your whole being – your joys, sorrows, fears, and hopes. Worship is a way of life, not something you do in a church building or during a worship service. In Psalm 34:1, David declares, *"I will bless the Lord at all times; his praise shall continually be in my mouth."*

You must understand that true worship goes beyond just singing. It involves obeying God's commands and living a life reflecting His character. Worship is about aligning your life with God's will. In worship, God always uses the opportunity to transform His beloved from the inside out, so you feel different after worshiping God.

In today's world, worship helps you focus on God, especially in times of trouble or uncertainty. As you worship, you experience His presence and peace more deeply. If you haven't already, cultivate a life of worship today. You will be glad you did. Here are chapters to help you get started:

- Psalm 8
- Psalm 19
- Psalm 29
- Psalm 33
- Psalm 47
- Psalm 66
- Psalm 95
- Psalm 96
- Psalm 100
- Psalm 150

Repentance

In the book of Psalms, you encounter people who are genuinely sorry for their mistakes, asking for God's forgiveness and seeking His help. Their encounters with God often lead to genuine repentance. Through their words, you understand what it means to have a heart fully committed to God and a profound love for Him.

Repentance is about turning back to God with a humble heart and seeking His forgiveness. As Christians, recognizing your mistakes when you err and asking God for a fresh start is essential. It is easy to go off track and make choices that do not align with God's will. Fortunately, the beautiful thing about God is He is always ready to forgive and welcome His beloved back when they come to Him with a sincere heart.

You cannot overlook the theme of repentance in the Psalms. It's all over the book. King David made sure of that. The Psalms show you that repentance involves consciously turning away from sin and walking in a new direction. King David prays in Psalm 51:10, *"Create in me a pure heart, O God, and renew a steadfast spirit within me."* He knew he could trust God to help him serve Him better.

In the book of Psalms, writers openly confess their sins and seek God's forgiveness. Repentance is being honest with God. You may deceive people around you, and sometimes, even yourself, through gaslighting, but you can never deceive God. He knows you better than you know yourself. True repentance begins with acknowledging the wrong you have done.

Psalm 32:5 says:

"Then I acknowledged my sin to you and did not cover up my iniquity. I said, 'I will confess my transgressions to the Lord.' And you forgave the guilt of my sin." 1 John 1:8-9, "If we claim to be without sin, we deceive ourselves and the truth is not in us. If we confess our sins, he is faithful and just and will forgive us our sins and purify us from all unrighteousness."

You cannot live a perfect life on your own. You will always need God's help to walk in righteousness. Repentance is one way to show God you depend on Him for grace and strength. God's love is greater than your failures, and His mercy is always available when you turn to Him with a repentant heart.

- Psalm 6
- Psalm 25
- Psalm 32
- Psalm 38
- Psalm 51
- Psalm 102
- Psalm 103
- Psalm 130
- Psalm 143
- Psalm 139

Seeking God's Guidance

Life is loaded with many uncertain moments, with overwhelming choices confusing you about your next line of action. You need God's guidance. The Psalms contain prayers acting as God's hotlines when you need guidance. Psalm 25:4-5 which says:

"Show me your ways, Lord, teach me your paths. Guide me in your truth and teach me, for you are God my Savior, and my hope is in you all day long."

Why do you need God's guidance? You did not create yourself. You easily make mistakes or choose a path far from His will. The Bible says in Proverbs 14:12, *"There is a way that appears to be right, but in the end leads to death."*

In Isaiah 48:21, the Bible also talks about how God does the impossible for His people when He leads them:

"They did not thirst when he led them through the deserts; he made water flow for them from the rock; he split the rock and water gushed out."

Who wouldn't want to be led by a God like that?

"He made water flow for them from the rock."[16]

Seeking God's guidance is essential. When you allow room for God's guidance, He directs your steps. He promised in Psalms 32:8:

"I will instruct you and teach you in the way you should go; I will counsel you with my loving eye on you."

God is always ready to guide you. Please note: you don't have to wait until you're lost before asking for His guidance. He wants to be involved in every decision you make, big or small. Make seeking His guidance daily a habit, and you will see how aligned you become with His will for your life.

- Psalm 5
- Psalm 16
- Psalm 23
- Psalm 25
- Psalm 32

- Psalm 48
- Psalm 73
- Psalm 143
- Psalm 139

Psalms Offering Wisdom and Encouragement

Wisdom Psalms

- Psalm 1
- Psalm 14
- Psalm 37
- Psalm 73
- Psalm 91
- Psalm 112
- Psalm 119
- Psalm 128

Psalms of Encouragement

Sometimes, you may feel like no one understands what you're going through. You might open up to a friend or loved one, hoping their advice will help you. God understands you better than anyone else. He made provision for the Psalms to encourage you whenever you feel left out or forsaken.

Here are 20 verses of encouragement from the Psalms:

- **Psalm 37:3-4, 7:** *"Trust in the Lord and do good; dwell in the land and enjoy safe pasture. Take delight in the Lord, and he will give you the desires of your heart. ... Be still before the Lord and wait patiently for him; do not fret when people succeed in their ways when they carry out their wicked schemes."*

- **Psalm 121:1-2:** *"I lift up my eyes to the mountains—where does my help come from? My help comes from the Lord, the Maker of heaven and earth."*

- **Psalm 23:4:** *"Even though I walk through the darkest valley, I will fear no evil, for you are with me; your rod and your staff, they comfort me."*

- **Psalm 27:1:** *"The Lord is my light and my salvation—whom shall I fear? The Lord is the stronghold of my life—of whom shall I be afraid?"*

- **Psalm 28:7:** *"The Lord is my strength and my shield; my heart trusts in him, and he helps me. My heart leaps for joy, and with my song I praise him."*

- **Psalm 31:24:** *"Be strong and take heart, all you who hope in the Lord."*

- **Psalm 34:4:** *"I sought the Lord, and he answered me; he delivered me from all my fears."*

- **Psalm 34:17-18:** *"The righteous cry out, and the Lord hears them; he delivers them from all their troubles. The Lord is close to the brokenhearted."*

- **Psalm 37:4:** *"Take delight in the Lord, and he will give you the desires of your heart."*

- **Psalm 37:5:** *"Commit your way to the Lord; trust in him*

- *and he will do this."*

- **Psalm 46:1:** *"God is our refuge and strength, an ever-present help in trouble."*

- **Psalm 55:22:** *"Cast your cares on the Lord and he will sustain you; he will never let the righteous be shaken."*

- **Psalm 56:3:** *"When I am afraid, I put my trust in you."*

- **Psalm 61:2:** *"From the ends of the earth I call to you, I call as my heart grows faint; lead me to the rock that is higher than I."*

- **Psalm 62:6:** *"Truly he is my rock and my salvation; he is my fortress; I will not be shaken."*

- **Psalm 91:2:** *"I will say of the Lord, 'He is my refuge and my fortress, my God, in whom I trust."*

- **Psalm 91:4:** *"He will cover you with his feathers, and under his wings, you will find refuge; his faithfulness will be your shield and rampart."*

- **Psalm 94:19:** *"When anxiety was great within me, your consolation brought me joy."*

- **Psalm 118:6:** *"The Lord is with me; I will not be afraid. What can mere mortals do to me?"*

- **Psalm 30:5:** *"For his anger lasts only a moment, but his favor lasts a lifetime; weeping may stay for the night, but rejoicing comes in the morning."*

God is deeply aware of all your thoughts, actions, and needs, and His presence constantly surrounds you. The book of Psalms encourages you to live with the assurance that you are never alone.

The Importance of Prayer and Meditation

Prayer and meditation are crucial in developing a solid spiritual life. Meditation, as in the Psalms, involves deeply pondering God's Word and His works. It helps you quiet your mind, connect with God, and gain clarity and strength for your daily life.

You must willingly set aside time for prayer and meditation in your daily life. For instance, King David's secret behind his victory and successful walk with God was prayer and meditation. When you pray, you speak to God and align your mind and heart with His Spirit.

Prayer has the power to transform your life entirely. When you pray regularly, you will notice a shift in your thinking. You become more positive, patient, and understanding. This shift doesn't happen overnight. However, you can create new, healthier patterns of thought, leading to better actions with consistent effort. Prayer helps you let go of the old ways that no longer serve you and become the woman God has purposed you to be.

Like Jesus sought solitude to pray and meditate, you, too, need this quiet time to renew your spirit. Life can be overwhelming with its many demands and distractions. But when you take time to be alone with God, you hear His voice more clearly and feel His presence more profoundly.

Prayer and meditation offer a unique opportunity. Together, as a power combo, they help you let go of worries, fears, and doubts. You gain renewed purpose and direction, knowing you no longer move through life blindly because God guides you, keeping you grounded in faith.

Timeless Relevance of the Psalms

The timeless relevance of the Psalms is evident in their connection to modern spiritual practices. They have existed for countless generations, offering comfort, wisdom, and inspiration. As you turn to a friend for advice or a shoulder to cry on, you can turn to the Psalms for guidance and solace.

The Psalms are incredibly relatable. Whether you feel overwhelmed, lost, or need a connection with something greater than yourself, the Psalms offer a comforting and familiar presence. They can help you express your deepest feelings to God. Sometimes, finding the right words to convey what's happening inside you is challenging. The Psalms provide a language allowing you to pour your heart out to the Lord your God.

The book of Psalms offers a timeless source of comfort, wisdom, and guidance. The more you study and use the Psalms, the more you deepen your connection with God and become empowered to live a more fulfilling life.

Journaling Prompt

Create a personal Psalm in your journal. Reflect on your spiritual journey and write a Psalm that expresses your prayers, praises, and reflections to God, inspired by the style and themes of the Biblical Psalms.

Chapter 6: Getting Closer to God Through the Gospels

Bible study aims to help you connect with God more profoundly. The entire sixty-six books of the Bible are God's attempt to bring Himself closer to His people. From the Old Testament to the New Testament, believers can experience God through numerous bible stories and understand how faithful He is to those He calls his own.

Since the beginning of this book, the Bible characters studied were from the Old Testament. Women who had never met Jesus nor His disciples yet still believed in the God of their fathers. The people of the Old Testament had no one to bring them the good news, but like Joshua, they and their households could choose to serve the Lord even amid confusion.

The New Testament is rich with Jesus' teachings and stories in the Gospels.[16]

This chapter centers on deepening and nurturing your relationship with God through Jesus' teachings and stories in the Gospels. So, it is time to explore books in the New Testament. This chapter aims to inspire you to follow the examples of Jesus and his disciples, fostering a closer and more personal connection with God.

The word *gospel* is derived from the Old English *Godspell*, which translates from the Greek word *euangelion*, meaning *good news* or *good telling*. This word described important news, like when a king won a battle or something good happened in the kingdom. The meaning of the word *gospel* became much deeper when Jesus came, over 400 years after the last book of the Old Testament was written. It became the perfect word for the special message Jesus brought to the world.

The Messiah came with a message of hope for people who felt lost or without help. He came to bring freedom to those who were suffering or feeling trapped. So, the word *gospel* became closely linked with the story of Jesus. Jesus and his disciples left the body of Christ with many interactions and examples to help shape the believers' minds into one fit for a glorious life with God.

The Core Teachings of the Gospels

The Gospels are the books in the Bible that tell about the life and ministry of Jesus. They were written to teach and show believers who Jesus was, what He did, and why He came. The Gospels center around the good news Jesus Christ came to share with the entire world. What was this good news? It is the message about God's unending love for mankind and how they could have a close relationship with Him.

Each Gospel provides a unique view of Jesus' life, His teachings, His miracles, and His compassion for people. The Gospels are the four accounts written by Jesus' disciples. It made sense to call them "Gospels" because they all shared the same good news that Jesus came to bring.

The first four books of the New Testament, Matthew, Mark, Luke, and John, are like four windows offering an insider's perspective of Jesus' life from different angles. Each highlights various aspects of Jesus' life and ministry, but they all portray his love for people and his desire to bring them closer to God.

Key Moments in Jesus' Ministry

The Sermon on the Mount

The sermon beginning with a blessing is God's way of assuring you of His unwavering promise of blessing. The aim is to remind you of His intention to bless you and His unfailing promises.

The Sermon on the Mount is in the book of Matthew, from chapter 5 to chapter 7. It was Jesus' longest teaching in the Gospels. The sermon laid out Jesus' moral vision for humanity. Jesus teaches a large crowd how to live if they want to follow God. He centered on humility, compassion, and forgiveness.

The sermon starts with the Beatitudes, a series of blessings describing the attitudes and actions that please God.

Matthew 5:1-12:

> *"Now when Jesus saw the crowds, he went up on a mountainside and sat down. His disciples came to him, and he began to teach them. He said: "Blessed are the poor in spirit, for theirs is the kingdom of heaven. Blessed are those who mourn, for they will be comforted. Blessed are the meek, for they will inherit the earth. Blessed are those who hunger and thirst for righteousness, for they will be filled. Blessed are the merciful, for they will be shown mercy. Blessed are the pure in heart, for they will see God. Blessed are the peacemakers, for they will be called children of God. Blessed are those who are persecuted because of righteousness, for theirs is the kingdom of heaven. Blessed are you when people insult you, persecute you, and falsely say all kinds of evil against you because of me. Rejoice and be glad because great is your reward in heaven, for in the same way they persecuted the prophets who were before you. "*

Beatitudes means a state of supreme happiness. So, this first part of the sermon was Jesus teaching the people that true happiness comes from living in a way that is pleasing to God. These mental states of mind became the blueprint for all who would become His disciples.

As He continued, Jesus referred to the believer as the light in a world of darkness and as the salt adding taste to the world around them:

"You are the salt of the earth. But if the salt loses its saltiness, how can it be made salty again? It is no longer good for anything except to be thrown out and trampled underfoot. You are the light of the world. A town built on a hill cannot be hidden. Neither do people light a lamp and put it under a bowl. Instead, they put it on its stand, and it gives light to everyone in the house. In the same way, let your light shine before others, that they may see your good deeds and glorify your Father in heaven." Matthew 5:13-16

He further tells them about acceptably fulfilling the law. He gave them a deeper understanding of God's commandments concerning murder (Matthew 5:21-25), adultery (Matthew 5:27-30), divorce (Matthew 5:31-32), oaths (Matthew 5:33-37), and vengeance (an eye for an eye) (Matthew 5:38-42).

Jesus taught that it is not enough to avoid murdering someone. He explained that if you are angry with someone without a good reason, you have broken the commandment because of murder in your heart.

Speaking on adultery, He said even looking at a person with lust is committing adultery in your heart. He admonished Christians to control what they do, think, and feel.

Think of what the world would be like if people truly obeyed these teachings, not only in their actions but also in their hearts. It would be like heaven. There would be no road rage, no shouting matches, no malice, no unnecessary violence, and no harsh words hurting others. People would be more patient and understanding and work hard to solve problems peacefully.

Instead of winning arguments, they would focus on finding solutions and making peace. If the commandment against lust were obeyed in spirit, there would be no infidelity, and marriages would be stronger and happier. Families would be more stable, and children would grow up in loving homes. There would be no need for pornography, etc. The industry would run out of business instead of flourishing like today. The world would be a much better place if everyone lived according to the law's spirit.

Jesus says to love those who mistreat you, forgive them, and pray for them.[17]

Also, Jesus gave the most difficult instructions to follow: *"Love your enemies"* (Matthew 5:44) and *"Be perfect, just as your Father in heaven is perfect"* (Matthew 5:48). God is perfect because God is love. Usually, when people are hurt, their first reaction is to hurt their offenders back or hold a grudge. However, Jesus says to love those who mistreat you, forgive them, and pray for them. This love is not easy, but it is the love God shows to all people.

God's love is unconditional. He cares deeply for everyone, even those who do not believe in Him or respect His name. He loves those who reject Him or use His name in vain. His love is not based on what you do or don't do. His love stems from His character and desire for everyone to know Him.

In Matthew 6, Jesus shifted the focus to trusting God and seeking His kingdom first. He tells the people not to worry about their daily needs, like food and clothing, because God knows what they need and will provide. He says, *"Seek first the kingdom of God and His righteousness, and all these things will be added to you"* Matthew 6:33.

Remember how the Bible says in Psalms 23:1, *"The Lord is my shepherd, I lack nothing,"* Psalms 34:10 says, *"The lions may grow weak and hungry, but those who seek the LORD lack no good thing."* Jesus was merely establishing what had been said centuries before Him. It shows that God is indeed faithful. When you seek and trust Him, He will bless you with every good thing.

The sermon included a session on being sincere in your actions and not only doing things to look good in front of others. Jesus talks about giving to the needy, praying, and fasting privately rather than doing these things to show off. God looks at the heart, and He values genuine devotion over outward appearances, 1 Samuel 16:17:

> *"But the LORD said unto Samuel, "Look not on his countenance or on the height of his stature, because I have refused him; for the LORD seeth not as man seeth. For man looketh on the outward appearance, but the LORD looketh on the heart."*

When you do good things quietly and sincerely, without seeking praise from others, it indicates your love for God is real and you are more concerned about what God thinks than what people think.

The Sermon on the Mount provides many lessons on how to live a life that is pleasing to God. You will learn to become humbler, loving, forgiving, and sincere if you study and meditate on it. You will grow closer to God and live in a way that reflects His love and righteousness.

Famous Parables

Jesus was famously known for speaking in *parables* in public places. It usually left the people confused. He did his best to explain them without using complex words. His disciples also had problems understanding His parables. So, He took His time to break it down, saying, *"...Because the knowledge of the secrets of the kingdom of heaven has been given to you, but not to them."* (Matthew 13:11).

But what does a parable mean? A parable is a simple story using everyday situations to illustrate a more profound spiritual truth. Some of the most famous parables Jesus told include:

The Parable of the Good Samaritan (Luke 10:29–37)

"But he wanted to justify himself, so he asked Jesus, "And who is my neighbor?" In reply, Jesus said: "A man was going down from Jerusalem to Jericho when he was attacked by robbers. They stripped him of his clothes, beat him, and went away, leaving him half dead. A priest happened to be going down the same road, and when he saw the man, he passed by on the other side. So, too, a Levite, when he came to the place and saw him, passed by on the other side. But a Samaritan, as he traveled, came where the man was; and when he saw him, he took pity on him. He went to him and bandaged his wounds, pouring on oil and wine. Then he put the man on his own donkey, brought him to an inn, and took care of him. The next day he took out two denarii and gave them to the innkeeper. 'Look after him,' he said, 'and when I return, I will reimburse you for any extra expense you may have.' "Which of these three do you think was a neighbor to the man who fell into the hands of robbers?" The expert in the law replied, "The one who had mercy on him." Jesus told him, "Go and do likewise."

In this story, a man is traveling from Jerusalem to Jericho when he is attacked by robbers, beaten, and left for dead. Several people pass by without helping him. Finally, a Samaritan — a person from Samaria whom the Jews did not like — bandages the man's wounds, takes him to an inn, and pays for his care. Jesus told this parable to encourage believers to act lovingly and caringly show kindness, compassion, and mercy to everyone because true neighborliness comes from the heart.

The Parable of the Prodigal Son (Luke 15:11-32)

"Jesus continued: "There was a man who had two sons. The younger one said to his father, 'Father, give me my share of the estate.' So, he divided his property between them. Not long after that, the younger son got together all he had, set off for a distant country and there squandered his wealth in wild living. After he had spent everything, there was a severe famine in that whole country, and he began to be in need. So, he went and hired himself out to a citizen of that country, who sent him to his fields to feed pigs. He longed to fill his stomach with the pods that the pigs were eating, but no one gave him anything. When he came to his senses, he said,

'How many of my father's hired servants have food to spare, and here I am starving to death! I will set out and go back to my father and say to him: Father, I have sinned against heaven and against you. I am no longer worthy to be called your son; make me like one of your hired servants.' So, he got up and went to his father. But while he was still a long way off, his father saw him and was filled with compassion for him; he ran to his son, threw his arms around him, and kissed him. The son said to him, 'Father, I have sinned against heaven and against you. I am no longer worthy to be called your son.' But the father said to his servants, 'Quick! Bring the best robe and put it on him. Put a ring on his finger and sandals on his feet. Bring the fattened calf and kill it. Let's have a feast and celebrate. For this son of mine was dead and is alive again; he was lost and is found.' So, they began to celebrate. Meanwhile, the older son was in the field. When he came near the house, he heard music and dancing. So, he called one of the servants and asked him what was going on. 'Your brother has come,' he replied, 'and your father has killed the fattened calf because he has him back safe and sound.' The older brother became angry and refused to go in. So, his father went out and pleaded with him. But he answered his father, 'Look! All these years I've been slaving for you and never disobeyed your orders. Yet you never gave me even a young goat so I could celebrate with my friends. But when this son of yours who has squandered your property with prostitutes comes home, you kill the fattened calf for him!' My son,' the father said, 'you are always with me, and everything I have is yours. But we had to celebrate and be glad because this brother of yours was dead and is alive again; he was lost and is found."

Like most people, the prodigal son wanted to live independently of his father. Jesus told this story to help people understand the depth of God's love. It didn't matter how long the son was gone, what he did with his father's money, or how he looked when he returned. His father readily received him with open arms and a kiss.

In the parable, the prodigal son represents people who have journeyed on their own, far from God. The father represents God, who is unconditional in His love. A God willing to accept you whenever you acknowledge your mistakes and return to Him. 1 John 1:9, "If we confess our sins, he is faithful and just and will forgive us our sins and purify us from all unrighteousness." Malachi 3:7:

"Ever since the time of your ancestors you have turned away from my decrees and have not kept them. Return to me, and I will return to you," says the Lord Almighty."

The Parable of the Lost Sheep (Luke 15:1-7)

"Now the tax collectors and sinners were all gathering around to hear Jesus. 2 But the Pharisees and the teachers of the law muttered, "This man welcomes sinners and eats with them." Then Jesus told them this parable: "Suppose one of you has a hundred sheep and loses one of them. Doesn't he leave the ninety-nine in the open country and go after the lost sheep until he finds it? And when he finds it, he joyfully puts it on his shoulders and goes home. Then he calls his friends and neighbors together and says, 'Rejoice with me; I have found my lost sheep.' I tell you that in the same way, there will be more rejoicing in heaven over one sinner who repents than over ninety-nine righteous persons who do not need to repent."

Jesus used this parable to explain how important every soul is to God. Leaving an entire flock of sheep to chase after one is not something many would do. But God is not man. He doesn't think like one. He wants all sinners to repent and draw close to Him. The Lord said in Ezekiel 18:23:

"Do I take any pleasure in the death of the wicked? Declares the Sovereign Lord. Rather, am I not pleased when they turn from their ways and live?"

Jesus used the lost sheep parable to explain how important every soul is to God.[18]

He was immensely fond of King David because, while tending to his father's sheep, David would chase and kill wild animals that tried to take his sheep. He could have run back home to tell his father that the lion and the bear attacked them. Instead, he kept the rest safe and chased after the animals because of one sheep. God loves all His children, and His mercy endures forever. Isaiah 43:4 says:

> *"Since you are precious and honored in my sight, and because I love you, I will give people in exchange for you, nations in exchange for your life."*

King David wrote a Psalm on God's love:

> *"Give thanks to the Lord, for he is good. His love endures forever. Give thanks to the God of gods. His love endures forever..."* Psalm 136

These are a few parables Jesus told. You can study many more during your Bible study.

- Parable of the Sower (Mark 4:1-20)
- Parable of the Pharisee and Publican (Luke 18:9-14)
- Parable of the Mustard Seed (Matthew 13:31-32)
- Parable of the Ten Virgins (Matthew 25:1-13)
- Parable of the Lost Coin (Luke 15:8-10)
- Parable of the Talents (Matthew 25:14-30)

Notable Miracles

The Feeding of the Five Thousand (Matthew 14:13-21)

The four gospels recount a miracle where Jesus fed five thousand people with only five loaves of bread and two fish. It was such a dramatic day. One moment, the disciples were anxious and worrying about how to feed the multitude. A thanksgiving prayer with five loaves of bread and two fishes later, Jesus performed a miracle.

Everyone ate until full, and there were leftovers. The disciples couldn't believe their eyes. This miracle was Jesus' way of showing the people that nothing was impossible with God. In Psalm 78:22-24, King David testified of God's ability to perform a miracle like this:

> *"...for they did not believe in God or trust in his deliverance. Yet he gave a command to the skies above and opened the doors of the heavens; he rained down manna for the people*

to eat, he gave them the grain of heaven." Read the original story in Exodus 16.

Always have faith in God's provision and be willing to share what you have. God can multiply your small offerings to meet greater needs in the blink of an eye. Matthew 19:26, *"...With man this is impossible, but with God all things are possible."*

Jesus Walking on Water (Matthew 14:22-32)

Have you ever looked at the ocean? Have you truly observed the ocean and watched how the water moves? What about its depth? Have you ever thought about the depth of an ocean? Water is larger than the entire land area on Earth. Water holds immense energy when it flows, which is called kinetic energy. Researchers learned that water covers over 70 percent of the Earth's surface, and 96.5 percent is seawater.

Now, with this context in mind, picture Jesus walking on water – not a fountain, a stream, a lake, or a river, but a sea. A sea! He did so with a calm and unbothered demeanor. He walked majestically like the King He is. He could have even been reading a scroll as He walked, paying no mind to the sea, only looking up to see He was on the right path to the boat as if it was an everyday activity. He asked Peter to come to Him, and Peter walked water until he allowed fear to cloud his mind.

With his unshakable faith in God, Jesus walked on water.[19]

This miracle happened after the feeding of the five thousand. Jesus sent His disciples ahead in a boat while He went up a mountain to pray. The disciples' boat was far from land during the night, and the wind was strong. Jesus came to them, walking on the water. The disciples were terrified, thinking He was a ghost, but Jesus reassured them, saying, *"Take courage! It is I. Don't be afraid."*

When Peter began to sink, Jesus reached out and caught him, saying, *"You of little faith, why did you doubt?"* Faith helps you overcome fear; however, it disguises itself. This miracle shows that Jesus will always help when you call out to Him.

The Woman with a Blood Issue

The story of the woman with the issue of blood is in three of the four gospels. This woman had suffered from this health challenge for over twelve years. Unlike the man at the pool of Bethesda, who had no one, the woman had people and money. She had been to the hospital several times, and presumably, doctors avoided her. Seeing a patient suffering from an illness you've tried over and over to cure is like a blow to your profession.

The woman spent all her money and time for more than 12 years looking for a solution to her predicament. All efforts were fruitless. One day, she heard Jesus was visiting the house of a synagogue leader in her area. She said to herself, *"If I just touch his clothes, I will be healed."* The miracle happened the moment she touched His garment. Suddenly, the blood dried up, and she was free.

Jesus felt power leave His body, and He perceived that someone with faith had touched Him – faith that was hard to ignore. He turned and asked, *"Who touched my clothes?"* But his disciples answered that it could have been anyone because a large crowd followed them. However, Jesus was no ordinary man. He knew it was someone special and kept looking.

The woman realized He would search until He found her, so she presented herself to Him. Jesus looked at her and smiled. He said to her, *"Daughter, your faith has healed you. Go in peace and be freed from your suffering."* This marked the end of her predicament.

What is that issue causing you heartache and distress? It doesn't matter how long or what the doctors call it. Jesus can heal you. Reach out to Him in faith today and receive your healing. In Isaiah 53:4, Prophet Isaiah prophesied about Jesus:

"Surely, he took up our pain and bore our suffering, yet we considered him punished by God, stricken by him, and afflicted. But he was pierced for our transgressions, he was crushed for our iniquities; the punishment

that brought us peace was on him, and by his wounds we are healed."

There are many other miracles in the gospels like these. Here are some you can study and meditate on later:

- The healing of the man born blind (John 9:1-12)
- The man at the pool of Bethesda (John 5:1-15)
- Turning water into wine (John 2:1-11)
- Raising Lazarus from the dead (John 11:1-43)
- Calming the storm (Mark 4:35-41)

Through these miracles, Jesus reveals the compassionate and powerful nature of God. When Jesus heals the sick, feeds the hungry, or raises the dead, He demonstrates His divine power and displays how active God is in the lives of those who trust and believe in Him.

Love, Compassion, and Forgiveness: Central Themes in the Gospels

In drawing closer to God, you cannot overemphasize the love, compassion, and forgiveness. Jesus admonishes believers to love each other as He loves them in John 13:34. Love is a spiritual force keeping God close to you. Chapter 4, on love and compassion, had more to say about this with scriptures and Bible characters who were agents of love and compassion.

Kindness or compassion is about noticing when someone needs help and helping them like Jesus did. It is not about noticing a problem and then going home to gossip about it with your friends. From the story of the Good Samaritan, you can see genuine kindness goes beyond what's typical or expected. The Good Samaritan helped a hurt stranger, even though they weren't of the same social status or culture. Showing kindness to loved ones and strangers is one way to live a Godly life, the life Christ lived.

Regarding forgiveness, Jesus teaches that you must forgive others to receive God's forgiveness (Matthew 6:14-15). Forgiveness frees you from the burden of bitterness and allows you to experience the fullness of God's grace. You feel lighter and more peaceful the moment you let go of anger or hurt. You reflect God's forgiving nature, which opens the door for deeper communion with Him if you practice forgiveness.

The Model for Discipleship and Spiritual Growth

Jesus' interactions with His disciples provide a model for discipleship and spiritual growth. He taught them through His words and by His example. He demonstrated how to live obediently to God, serve others, and remain faithful even in challenges. He imbibed in them the vital characteristics of true leadership: service, humility, and love.

Jesus called them to be with Him, to learn from Him, and to support one another. They were His family, friends, and community. A community like that is essential for nurturing a relationship with God because it provides encouragement, accountability, and a shared faith experience. So, even as you pursue spiritual growth, keep room for creating or joining a community that loves God like you do. You can learn from each other's experiences and encounters with God.

Journaling Prompt

Create a weekly devotion plan based on the Gospels. Each day, read a passage from the Gospels you wrote about in your journal (make it stand out by adding creativity), reflect on its meaning, and write down how you can apply it to your life. Use this practice to nurture and strengthen your relationship with God.

Chapter 7: Women of the Gospel: The Stories of Mary and Mary Magdalene

After exploring the four gospels, it is a good time to read stories of notable women of the gospels. Unlike the Old Testament, which referred to many women and their impact on God's purpose for the Israelites, the New Testament only mentions a few.

The New Testament celebrated more men than women – Jesus' closest disciples were men. However, whenever a crowd listened to Jesus, the women were more in attendance than men, which is still evident today. If you enter a well-populated church, you will notice most members are women. They may not always take up a leadership role – but they are always present where Jesus is.

The New Testament also tells stories of two women who stood out in Jesus' ministry.[20]

This character-based chapter focuses on the stories and profiles of two women who stood out in Jesus' ministry – how they met Him, grew in faith as they listened to His teachings, became disciples and loyal followers, and followed Him until His death and after His resurrection.

More interestingly, they have the same name. You've probably guessed it already. So, are you down for more Bible character study? If yes, then keep reading.

Mary | The Mother of Jesus

Mary, the mother of Jesus, was an average young lady next door – quiet, calm, beautiful, kept to herself, and faithful to God and her fiancé. When Mary got engaged, she was still a virgin and an exemplary, nice young woman. Many men clamored to woo her. However, the lucky man was Joseph, a decent, humble, and God-fearing man.

Joseph came from King David's lineage, born and raised in a small town of Nazareth in Galilee. His ancestors were Abraham, Isaac, Jacob, Judah, Jesse, etc. He had a high-paying job in carpentry and was comfortably well-off. Unlike some of the men in the town, he didn't want to fool around with just any woman. He knew Mary was the one for him and wanted to make her an honest wife.

Their relationship was the talk of the town. They were perfect for each other. However, Joseph made a shocking discovery with the wedding date approaching fast. Mary was pregnant! His virgin fiancée was pregnant.

How did this happen? The Book of Luke records that the angel Gabriel visited Mary. Luke 1:26-35,:

> *"The angel came to her and said, "You are honored very much. You are a favored woman. The Lord is with you. You are chosen from among many women." When she saw the angel, she was troubled by his words. She thought about what had been said. The angel said to her, "Mary, do not be afraid. You have found favor with God. See! You are to become a mother and have a Son. You are to give Him the name Jesus. He will be great. He will be called the Son of the Most High. The Lord God will give Him the place where His early father David sat. He will be King over the family of Jacob forever and His nation will have no end." Mary said to the angel, "How will this happen? I have never had a man." The angel said to her, "The Holy Spirit will come on you. The power of*

the Most High will cover you. The holy Child you give birth
to will be called the Son of God."

Although shocked and confused, Mary, as always, willingly served God's purpose. Her heart raced when the angel left her. How would she tell Joseph? What would she tell him? What about her family? Joseph's family? How could she explain becoming pregnant overnight? What does she tell her best friend? The questions kept rolling through her mind, but then she remembered the word of the Lord from the angel: *"Do not be afraid. You have found favor with God."*

So, Mary steeled herself and kept her emotions in check. God would not put her to shame. She knew Him as faithful and just. Even though she was young, she had dedicated her life to serving the Lord. God heard her thoughts and noted her worries, so he sent an angel to speak to Joseph.

Joseph, respecting the laws of the land prepared to break the engagement. The child was not his, so he shouldn't be the one marrying Mary. He decided to do it quietly so as to not hurt Mary's image. While planning to let her go, an angel visited him in a dream and explained the situation. Matthew 1:20-21:

> *"While he was thinking about this, an angel of the Lord came to him in a dream. The angel said, "Joseph, son of David, do not be afraid to take Mary as your wife. She is to become a mother by the Holy Spirit. A Son will be born to her. You will give Him the name Jesus because He will save His people from the punishment of their sins."*

After the angel's visit, Joseph knew what to do. He quickly married Mary and assisted her throughout the pregnancy. Mary thanks God for choosing her in Luke 1:46-55:

> *"Then Mary said, "My heart sings with thanks for my Lord. And my spirit is happy in God, the One Who saves from the punishment of sin. The Lord has looked on me, His servant-girl and one who is not important. But from now on all people will honor me. He Who is powerful has done great things for me. His name is Holy. The loving-kindness of the Lord is given to the people of all times who honor Him. He has done powerful works with His arm. He has divided from each other those who have pride in their hearts. He has taken rulers down from their thrones. He has put those who are in a place that is not important to a place that is important. He*

has filled those who are hungry with good things. He has sent the rich people away with nothing. He has helped Israel His servant. This was done to remember His loving-kindness. He promised He would do this to our early fathers and to Abraham and to his family forever."

After seeing that God had opened Elizabeth's womb like the angel said, reality dawned on Mary, and she couldn't contain her joy.

When Jesus started His ministry at the wedding in Cana, Mary told the servants, *"Whatever He tells you, do it"* John 2:5. Mary knew exactly who Jesus was and what He could do. He did not disappoint.

When Jesus' ministry on Earth ended, it was time to say goodbye to his human form at the cross. Mary was gripped with grief. She had watched Him grow from a tiny baby wrapped in swaddling clothes to the wounded and bruised man hanging on the cross as was prophesied about Him. Mary was sad but grateful. God's will be done, and she had played her part in it.

Mary Magdalene | The Woman Disciple

Mary Magdalene is another Mary featured in Jesus' life, and her presence wasn't fleeting. She was first introduced in Luke 8:1-3, *"After this, Jesus traveled about from one town and village to another, proclaiming the good news of the kingdom of God. The Twelve were with him, and also some women who had been cured of evil spirits and diseases: Mary (called Magdalene) from whom seven demons had come out; Joanna, the wife of Chuza, the manager of Herod's household; Susanna; and many others. These women were helping to support them out of their own means."*

Mary Magdalene, a close follower of Jesus, loved and believed in Him immensely.[21]

The Bible records that she was one of the women who traveled with Jesus and supported His ministry with her finances. All the gospels had something to say about her because of her dedication and activeness in Jesus' ministry.

Mary Magdalene, a close follower of Jesus, loved and believed in Him immensely. At Jesus' crucifixion, she was there. It was sad and heartbreaking because Jesus, who had taught much about love and kindness, was treated so cruelly. Most people who gathered at the cross to witness the crucifixion left the scene after a while, but Mary stayed because she wanted to be close to Jesus. She witnessed His suffering until He died. Standing near the cross, Mary watched Jesus speak His last words. She saw the sky turn dark, felt the earth shake, and experienced everything that happened afterward.

When soldiers came to take Jesus' body away, she made sure to locate where He was buried. She and other women wanted to ensure His body was cared for, so they planned to return back after the Sabbath. Early Sunday morning, while it was still dark, Mary Magdalene went to the tomb. She wanted to put special spices on Jesus' body, as was the custom. When she arrived, Mary saw the huge stone covering the tomb's entrance had rolled away! Confused and thinking someone might have taken Jesus' body, she ran to tell the disciples, Peter and John. They came to see for themselves.

As she wept, Mary looked into the tomb again. This time, she saw two angels dressed in white sitting where Jesus' body had been. They asked her:

"Why are you crying?"

She answered:

"They have taken my Lord away, and I don't know where they have put Him."

Then she turned around and saw a man standing there whom she thought was a gardener (John 20:13-14).

Then, the man said her name, "Mary." At that moment, Mary realized it was Jesus speaking. He was alive! Her heart must have leaped with joy. Jesus told her to go and tell the others that He had risen from the dead. Mary Magdalene ran to tell the disciples the amazing news. She couldn't wait to share that Jesus had risen like He said He would. She was the first person to see Jesus alive. She was so excited to share this miracle with everyone.

There is a common misconception about Mary Magdalene being a prostitute. The Bible does not explicitly say that Mary Magdalene was a prostitute. It only records the one time when Jesus cast out seven demons from her (Luke 8:2). Some people believe Mary Magdalene was the same person as another unnamed woman in the Bible, who many thought was a prostitute and is known for washing Jesus' feet with her tears and drying them with her hair (Luke 7:36-38). However, there is no evidence that these two women are the same person.

Lessons from Their Lives

Faith and Obedience

Mary demonstrated deep faith and obedience by accepting God's will for her life, even when facing uncertainty and potential shame. Her response to angel Gabriel's message was trust and submission, saying, *"I am the Lord's servant...May your word to me be fulfilled"* (Luke 1:38). She accepted her role as Jesus' mother, trusting in God's plan despite the challenges that would come with it. Her faith was steadfast, and she remained obedient to God's call. Mary became the perfect example of trusting God's purpose, even when you do not fully understand the circumstances.

Mary Magdalene's faith and obedience were evident in her unwavering support for Jesus throughout His ministry. Mary Magdalene followed Jesus faithfully despite her past, providing for Him and His disciples. She embraced her role with devotion. Her faith led to her transformation and a new purpose.

Courage and Perseverance

Mary, Jesus' mother, showed immense courage when she accepted the angel's message that she would bear the Son of God. She faced potential disgrace, misunderstanding, and rejection from her community, yet she willingly obeyed God. She persevered through her personal pain, trusting in God's greater plan.

Mary, Jesus' mother, showed immense courage when she accepted the angel's message that she would bear the Son of God.[23]

Mary Magdalene's courage is highlighted by her presence at Jesus' crucifixion when many others fled in fear. She persevered in her devotion to Jesus, even when He was no longer physically present. She displayed courage by going to the tomb to honor Jesus' body. She did not let fear or societal judgment deter her from her devotion.

Devotion and Service

Virgin Mary's devotion is seen throughout Jesus' life, from His birth to His death. She cared for Him, supported His ministry, and followed Him to the very end. She was wholly humble with a profound purpose. Even at the wedding in Cana, she demonstrated her faith in Jesus by encouraging others to follow His instructions, showing her ongoing devotion and service to His mission.

Mary Magdalene's devotion is evident in her financial support of Jesus' ministry and constant presence with Him. She followed Jesus and served His mission actively, providing for Him and His disciples. Her devotion was unwavering, and she was among the first to witness His resurrection. She was entrusted with the task of delivering the news to the disciples.

Witness and Proclamation

Mary, Jesus' mother, was crucial as a witness to Jesus' life, death, and resurrection. She witnessed Jesus' first miracle at the wedding in Cana and was present during His crucifixion. Her life and actions proclaimed her faith and trust in God's plan, making her a powerful witness to God's work in the world.

Mary Magdalene: Mary Magdalene was the first to witness the risen Christ and was tasked with proclaiming this incredible news to the disciples. She became the first evangelist because she saw Jesus' resurrection. She boldly shared the news despite the potential disbelief and shock from others – she was too excited to care.

Mary, Jesus' mother and her namesake from Magdala, boldly shared their faith and experiences with others. Witnessing God's work and declaring your faith openly can inspire and encourage others to do the same.

Journaling Prompt

Reflect on a time in your life when you felt called to step out in faith like Mary, Jesus' mother, when she accepted God's plan for her life. How did you respond to that calling? What fears or uncertainties did you face? How did you overcome them? Consider Mary Magdalene's example, who demonstrated unwavering devotion and courage even in great challenges. How can you incorporate similar faithfulness and dedication into your daily life?

Chapter 8: Discovering Your God-Given Purpose

Have you ever heard the saying, "When the purpose of a thing is not known, abuse is inevitable"? This means you might misuse something if you don't know what it is intended for. For instance, say you have an awesome smartphone with fantastic camera quality, but you only use it to take blurry selfies. Why? You don't know all the neat tricks and features that come with the phone. You're missing out on the fun and incredible photos you could take because you don't understand the purpose of those little buttons and settings.

Imagine your smartphone is like a Swiss Army knife. You know, the one with the tiny tools that fold out—scissors, bottle openers, screwdrivers, the whole shebang. If you only ever use the knife, you're not getting the full potential. Right? The scissors would cut things, the bottle opener would open a soda, and the screwdriver would fix things around the house. Your new knife might have all these options, but that's not very efficient if you don't know all the tools for using the knife for everything.

Discovering your God-given purpose gives your life a deeper meaning.[38]

The same thing happens with humans. If you don't know your purpose, you might feel like that Swiss Army knife is only used to cut string. So, you only do things. You might not feel as happy or fulfilled because you don't do what you were truly meant to do. Learning what it is is like discovering that your smartphone camera has a slow-motion feature. Suddenly, life becomes a lot more exciting and meaningful.

This chapter will guide you through essential steps to help find and develop your God-given purpose. God-given, because everyone created and born comes for a reason or with a particular built-in skill set they only need to discover and harness. A section features biblical examples of characters discovering and fulfilling their God-given purpose.

If you struggle to find yours, this is your chance to look inward and uncover your unique, God-given purpose through this chapter's biblical teachings and examples.

If you're not in this category, that's fine. Read for a friend. If you don't have any friends, read anyway, you'll learn a thing or two.

The Concept of Divine Purpose and Its Significance in a Believer's Life

Like every strong and powerful building constructed according to the appropriate professional's architectural design, humans follow a blueprint to make the most of their lives. Every person is created for a unique reason, known as their divine purpose. This divine purpose is God's exclusive blueprint or plan for each individual.

This plan fits perfectly with who you are, your abilities, passions, and challenges because God is the architect. Like a piece in a puzzle has its perfect place, each person has a special role in God's big picture. However, it may take time to discover and understand this plan. The Lord says in Isaiah 55:8-9, *"For my thoughts are not your thoughts, neither are your ways my ways,"* declares the LORD. "As the heavens are higher than the earth, so are my ways higher than your ways and my thoughts than your thoughts.

God's purpose for your life is something He planned long before you were born. Jeremiah 1:5:

> *"Before I formed you in the womb I knew you, before you were born I set you apart; I appointed you as a prophet to the nations."*

He knows every detail about your life and has a reason for each step you take.

Understanding your divine purpose gives your life meaning and direction. When you discover what God wants you to do, you will feel peace and joy because you know you walk the path He has set for you. As rewarding and fulfilling as discovering your divine purpose can be, it is not always easy. It requires much patience and faith. Don't worry. The practical steps to discover and develop your God-given purpose are laid out in this chapter. First, here are a few biblical examples to learn from.

Biblical Figures Who Discovered and Fulfilled Their God-Given Purposes

The Bible has many stories of people who discovered their divine purpose and followed it with all their hearts. Finding and fulfilling your purpose is not always easy, but it is worth it. The following stories illustrate the significance of finding your God-given purpose:

Moses As a Leader

Moses is one of the most well-known figures in the Bible. He is known as the man whom God spoke to face to face. Exodus 33:11,

> *"The Lord would speak to Moses face to face, as one speaks to a friend. Then Moses would return to the camp, but his young aide Joshua son of Nun did not leave the tent."*

Imagine being Moses, growing up in a palace with all the riches and education you could desire. You are raised as an Egyptian prince, but you know you're different deep inside. Your people, the Israelites, do not live in palaces and don't have the same privileges as you.

One day, you see an Egyptian beating an Israelite man. In the heat of the moment, your passion flares up. You can't stand to see this injustice, so you step in and defend the Israelites, striking down the Egyptians. It might seem like a single act of anger, but it is a sign of the leader you are meant to become. God reveals your purpose, even if you don't fully understand it yet. You strongly desire to protect your people, stand up for them, and fight against their oppression.

However, you don't immediately become a respected leader – you had to flee from Egypt because of what you did. You end up in the desert, far from everything you ever knew. Yet, this is where God prepares you for greatness. Sometimes, you must go through hard times to understand what you are truly meant to do. In the quiet and stillness of the desert, God speaks to you. He shows you a burning bush, but the leaves stand tall like Shadrach, Meshach, and Abednego in the fiery furnace. God tells you to lead your people out of slavery. Finally, you know God's purpose for you—to be a deliverer.

So, you see, finding your purpose isn't always straightforward. Sometimes, it begins with a strong feeling or passion you care deeply about. You might not see the whole picture right away. For Moses, his anger over injustice became the first hint.

His God-given assignment wasn't a walk in the park. It was certainly not for the faint-hearted. Fortunately, Moses chose faith over fear and obeyed God. He returned to Egypt, confronted the Pharaoh, and performed miracles using God's power to show that God was real and powerful. God empowered Moses to lead the Israelites out of Egypt and across the Red Sea, where God performed a miracle by parting the waters so they could cross safely.

Moses led the people through the desert for 40 years, teaching them about God's laws and how to live as His people. Through it all, Moses fulfilled his divine purpose by trusting God and leading his people with courage and faith.

Esther, As a Queen

If someone had told Esther she would become queen of the Persian Empire while she and her people were exiled, she would probably suggest they nap to rest their heads.

Esther's story is a powerful example of how God can use anyone to fulfill a divine purpose, no matter how unlikely. Esther was the daughter of a Benjaminite, Abihail. Her parents died when she was young, so her uncle, Mordecai, took custody of her. By a miraculous twist of fate, the king of the Persian Empire removed his wife from the palace, and the search for a new wife began.

Esther wouldn't have believed she'd be the queen of the Persian Empire.⁴

Esther was chosen from among many young women. It seemed like a great honor, but it also put Esther in a difficult position. She had to hide her Jewish identity because to be a Jew in the king's palace was dangerous. That was risk number one.

Soon after Esther became queen, a wicked man named Haman, a high official in the king's court, became angry with Mordecai because Mordecai would not bow down to him. In his anger, Haman tricked the king into making a law to destroy all the Jews in the kingdom.

When Mordecai heard about this, he was highly upset and sent a message to Esther, asking her to go to the king and beg for their lives. Esther knew that going to the king without an invitation could mean death. However, Mordecai reminded her that she might be queen to save her people. Esther 4:14, *"For if you remain silent at this time, relief and deliverance for the Jews will arise from another place, but you and your father's family will perish. And who knows but that you have come to a royal position for such a time as this?"*

Esther had to be brave to take risk number two. She fasted and prayed for three days and asked the Jews to do the same. Esther 4:16, *"Go, gather together all the Jews who are in Susa, and fast for me. Do not eat or drink for three days, night or day. I and my maids will fast as you do. When this is done, I will go to the king, even though it is against the law. And if I perish, I perish."* She put on her royal robes and went to see the king. God gave her favor in the king's eyes, and he allowed her to speak. Esther invited the king and Haman to a banquet, and at the banquet, she revealed her Jewish identity and told the king about Haman's evil plan. The king was furious and ordered Haman to be punished. Ester's divine purpose saved the Jews.

Esther fulfilled her divine purpose by being courageous and trusting God. Her bravery saved her people and showed that God can use anyone to fulfill His plans, no matter how difficult the situation may seem.

Paul the Apostle

Paul, known as Saul, had a different story. Initially, he was not a follower of Jesus. He did not believe in Jesus, and those who followed Him were wrong.

Paul strictly followed the Jewish laws and believed the followers of Jesus broke those laws. He went as far as to hunt down Christians, imprisoning and torturing them. Acts 9:1-2, *"Meanwhile, Saul was still breathing out murderous threats against the Lord's disciples. He went to the high priest and asked him for letters to the synagogues in Damascus so that if he found any there who belonged to the Way, whether men or women, he might take them as prisoners to Jerusalem."* Paul thought he was doing the right thing. However, he fought against God's true purpose.

One day, Paul was on his way to Damascus to arrest more Christians, and something incredible happened. A bright light from heaven suddenly shone around him, and he fell to the ground. He heard a voice saying, *"Saul, Saul, why do you persecute me?"* Jesus spoke to him from heaven. Shocked and terrified, Paul asked, *"Who are you, Lord?"* Jesus replied, *"I am Jesus, whom you are persecuting"* (Acts 9:3-6). This encounter completely changed Paul's life. He realized Jesus was real and he had been wrong.

After this encounter, Paul became a follower of Jesus. He understood his purpose was to tell everyone about Jesus and the good news of salvation. Paul traveled to many places, preaching about Jesus, starting churches, and helping believers grow in their faith. His path came with immense challenges – he was imprisoned, beaten, faced many dangers, and even shipwrecked.

However, Paul knew he was doing God's will and continued with vigor. He wrote many letters to the Churches, now part of the Bible. He used the letters to teach and encourage Christians to continue their faith.

Apostle Paul dedicated his life to sharing the gospel of Jesus Christ and God's love and excelled because this was his divine purpose.

Understanding Your Divine Purpose

Like Moses, Esther, and Paul, every believer has a divine purpose, a unique role God planned for them to fulfill. Discovering this purpose is not easy and usually takes time. Sometimes, you must go through difficult situations to grow and learn more about yourself and God's plan for you. These challenges help shape and prepare you for God's tasks. God's purpose for everyone is always good. Jeremiah 29:11, *"For I know the plans I have for you," declares the LORD, "plans to prosper you and not to harm you, plans to give you hope and a future."*

You must stay close to God to find your divine purpose. God gives you hope and a future. Spending time in prayer, reading the Bible, and talking to other believers who can provide you with sound advice and support will guide you to your divine purpose. Pay attention to what you are naturally drawn to and what you enjoy doing and are good at. Sometimes, God speaks to you through your desires and talents to guide you toward living a life full of joy and fulfillment to help others.

You can't discover your divine purpose and then relax. You must catch and run with the vision, or you will be like the man who keeps the talent hidden. Matthew 25:24-28:

"Then the man who had received one bag of gold came. 'Master,' he said, 'I knew that you are a hard man, harvesting where you have not sown and gathering where you have not scattered seed. So, I was afraid and went out and hid your gold in the ground. See, here is what belongs to you.' His master replied, 'You wicked, lazy servant! So, you knew that I harvest where I have not sown and gather where I have not scattered seed? Well then, you should have put my money on deposit with the bankers, so that when I returned I would have received it back with interest." So, take the bag of gold from him and give it to the one who has ten bags. For whoever has will be given more, and they will have an abundance. Whoever does not have, even what they have will be taken from them."

You can see how dangerous it is to find your purpose and sit on it. Once you find your purpose, don't let anyone tell you otherwise. Follow it with all your heart, like Moses, Esther, and Paul did. Everyone has their unique path. Sometimes, finding and following God's purpose might require leaving close friends or loved ones, but you must be ready to do so. It could mean joining forces with people you never imagined speaking to, but you're not the one in charge. God is. 1 Thessalonians 5:24, "The one who calls you is faithful, and he will do it."

You might face challenges and difficulties, but you can trust that God is with you, helping you and giving you strength. He promised to never leave nor forsake you. He will help you fulfill your destiny.

Practical Steps for Identifying and Developing Your God-Given Purpose

Finding your God-given purpose is a big deal. But don't worry. This section breaks it down into small, easy, practical steps. In the quest to find your purpose, you must look at the clues: your strengths, passions, and experiences. Guess what? God plants tiny hints around you from the time you're born to help you figure it out. Here's where to look for:

God plants tiny seeds in your life that reveal your life purpose.[25]

Look at the Things You Naturally Excel In

The first place to check is what you're naturally good at—your strengths. These are things that come easily to you, maybe things you don't notice because they feel like second nature. Do your friends compare you to a famous singer because of how well you sing at home? Can you whip up a delicious meal without breaking a sweat (and without burning the kitchen down—bonus points for that)? Perhaps you have an excellent memory and reproduce an image you see on paper with intricate details, or maybe you are the best at organizing things. These are hints as to your true purpose.

You might think, "But I'm not good at anything." Here's a secret you should know for free: everyone has something they excel in, including you. It might be something small, like always being on time (not everyone has that gift) or a talent for making people laugh. Think about what people compliment you on or what comes naturally to you. Write them down. You could be on to something with those clues.

What Are You Passionate About?

For Moses, he was ready to fight for his people. For Paul, he was ready to die for what he believed in. Now, ask yourself, what is one thing that sets your heart on fire? What could you talk about for hours without getting bored? What makes you come alive? When God calls you, He often starts with something that already stirs your heart. Your passion is not random. It's a clue to what you are meant to do. Like Moses, you might go through a desert period of waiting and preparation. Time doesn't necessarily mean delay. It is God shaping and preparing you for your purpose. Your passions are another signpost pointing you toward your God-given purpose.

Consult Your Yesterdays

This is something not everyone does. Most people are all about the present and moving toward the future, living like yesterday never existed. However, in the quest to find your purpose, you must visit your past. So, try something in this 'now moment.' Look back at your life. Sometimes, thinking about the past is not fun, especially if it is mostly unpleasant. However, your experiences shape you.

Everything that happened then was no accident. God uses everything. Think about the good, the bad, and the funny (like when you tried to dye your hair and ended up with a color not found in nature). What did you learn from the experiences? How have they made you stronger, wiser, or more compassionate? Write these down because they will guide you toward your purpose.

Step Out, Try Something New and Explore

This is where it gets exciting. Once you've done some soul-searching, it's time to act. The wisest man in the Bible said in Proverbs 14:23, *"All hard work brings a profit, but mere talk leads only to poverty."* It's not enough to wonder about your purpose and keep talking about it. Start trying new things! Your purpose may be something you haven't tried yet. Maybe you admire people who do it. Explore while you still have the time. If you think you might be called to help others, volunteer somewhere. If you feel a pull toward creativity, start painting or writing. Don't be afraid to step out of your comfort zone. Your God-given purpose won't pay you a surprise visit if all you do is sit on the couch and watch TV all day. Come out of your cocoon.

Pray and Ask God for Guidance

This is the most important step. Miss this one, and you might miss your way. The Bible records in Proverbs 14:12, *"There is a way that appears to be right but in the end, it leads to death."* God must be involved. As a human, your knowledge and power are limited. The good news is that you don't have to figure it out by yourself. Isn't that a relief? God will guide you. He knows your purpose. So, use quiet time to pray and ask Him to show you the way.

When you pray, be honest with God. Tell Him about your worries, hopes, and confusions. The answer could come in several ways: feeling peaceful, a new idea, or a conversation with a friend. Keep your heart open and trust that God is leading you where you need to go.

Prayer is crucial to discovering your God-given purpose. You must pray frequently, ask God for guidance, and listen carefully to His voice during your purpose-discovering journey. It can happen through reading the Bible, talking with other believers, or paying attention to what you feel passionate about. God often speaks quietly through your thoughts, feelings, and people around you. There will be more about prayer in the next and final chapter.

As you grow in your relationship with Him, He will reveal more of His plan for you. When you finally understand your purpose, it changes everything about how you live. You're expected to make choices in line with God's plan, giving you peace knowing you're doing what you were born for.

Journaling Prompt

Create a purpose vision board in your journal. Gather images, quotes, and Bible verses that resonate with your understanding of your God-given purpose. Arrange them on a board to create a visual representation of your calling. Use this board as a daily reminder to stay focused on your divine purpose.

Chapter 9: Developing a Consistent Prayer Life

Many believers make the mistake of only praying to God when in need or afraid. Remembering to pray when facing a problem too big to handle or when scared and unsure is easy. In times like this, you quickly pour your heart out, telling Him about your troubles, fears, and worries because you desperately seek His intervention.

While it's good to pray in these times because God wants you to bring your needs and fears to Him, prayer is much more than a tool for emergencies or solving your problems. Prayer is a way to build a deep and personal relationship with God.

Praying consistently enriches your relationship with God.[36]

Imagine if you only talked to a close friend when you needed something or were afraid. The relationship would feel shallow and one-sided, wouldn't it? The same is true with God. He desires a relationship with you based on more than your needs. God wants you to come to Him in all situations. 1 Peter 5:7, *"Cast all your anxiety on him because he cares for you."* It doesn't matter if you're happy, sad, joyful, or grieving. He wants to always fellowship with you.

Making time to pray and study the bible regularly is telling the Lord you value your relationship with Him. Tell him everything. He will listen and help you. Developing a consistent prayer life tells God you want to know Him more deeply, not because of what He can do for you, but because of who He is. God knows you're using Him only for the one-issue-to-worry-about prayer. Instead, consciously seek Him daily, spend time in His presence, and talk to Him about everything. You will build a rich and lasting relationship with your Heavenly Father, brick by brick.

This chapter will help you develop a consistent prayer life because you'll need it while searching for and developing your God-given purpose.

Benefits of Regular Pray and Bible Study

Increase in Faith Level

Praying and reading the Bible daily helps your faith grow stronger, like exercising makes your body stronger. The more you learn about God's love and promises, the more you trust Him. You saw how God helped people in the Bible. Start believing He can help you, too. Whenever you pray, you're showing trust in God and building faith over time. Romans 10:17, *"So then faith comes by hearing, and hearing by the word of God."* Hebrews 11:6, *"And without faith, it is impossible to please God, because anyone who comes to Him must believe that He exists and that He rewards those who earnestly seek Him."*

Increase in Peace

Regular prayer and Bible study bring peace into your life. When you pray, you give your worries and problems to God, like handing over a heavy bag to someone to carry it. Reading the Bible reminds you of God's promises and care for you, helping you feel calmer and less stressed. You feel peace, knowing God is always with you. Philippians 4:6-7:

"Do not be anxious about anything, but in every situation, by prayer and petition, with thanksgiving, present your requests to God. And the peace of God, which transcends all understanding, will guard your hearts and your minds in Christ Jesus."

Isaiah 26:3:

"You will keep in perfect peace those whose minds are steadfast because they trust in you."

Increase in Guidance

If you cultivate the habit of praying (asking God) for guidance, you will see how real God is in your life. Jeremiah 33:3 says, *"Call to me and I will answer you and tell you great and unsearchable things you do not know."* You ask for guidance because you do not know. God can show you the right path, the best decisions, and the people who will help you grow. Regular Bible study enables you to understand God's guidance better. Psalm 119:105, *"Your word is a lamp for my feet, a light on my path."* When you read the Bible often, you learn about what God wants for your life. You start to feel more confident in knowing what to do.

Biblical Examples of People with a Disciplined Prayer Life

Daniel

Daniel was a man in the Old Testament with a disciplined prayer life. The Bible states that Daniel prayed to God three times daily, kneeling by his window facing Jerusalem (Daniel 6:10). It was a habit he would not break even if his life depended on it. He continued to pray even when the king made a law that anyone who prayed to anyone other than the king would be thrown into a den of lions. But he wasn't afraid. Like he said in Daniel 11:32, *"...but the people who know their God shall stand firm and take action."* (ESV)

Jesus

Jesus is the perfect role model of a disciplined prayer life. Even though He had a very busy life, He made time to pray for an hour or more. Jesus traveled about teaching people, healing the sick, and performing miracles, yet He prayed regularly. He often went to quiet places early in the morning or late at night to pray to His Father in heaven. Mark 1:35:

"Very early in the morning, while it was still dark, Jesus got up, left the house, and went off to a solitary place, where he prayed."

Matthew 14:23:

"After he had dismissed them, he went up on a mountainside by himself to pray. Later that night, he was there alone."

Luke 6:12:

"One of those days Jesus went out to a mountainside to pray, and spent the night praying to God."

The Early Christians

The early Christians were the multitude who followed Jesus wherever He went. So, when He ascended to heaven, they would come together as a group, often meeting in each other's homes to share meals and pray. The Bible says they were *"Devoted to the apostles' teaching and to fellowship, to the breaking of bread and to prayer"* (Acts 2:42). They were very committed to spending time together, learning more about God, and praying. In Acts 12:5-7, they prayed fervently, and an angel rescued Peter.

Practical Tips for Creating a Prayer Schedule

Setting Specific Times for Prayer

When will you most likely have a few quiet minutes throughout your day? Is it early in the morning before the house wakes up or in the evening after the kids are in bed? Find a time that works best for you, and try to stick to it every day. Setting a regular time helps make prayer a habit. You might start with praying in the morning when you wake up or praying at night as the last thing you do before bed. Or it could be both.

Setting Specific Places for Prayer

Just as having a specific time is important, it can also help to have a special place for prayer. This should be somewhere you feel comfortable and can focus on talking to God. It could be a corner of your bedroom, a cozy chair in your living room, or a spot in your garden. The aim is to ensure you don't get distracted. It helps you feel closer to God because it's just you and Him in that moment.

Methods of Prayer

Prayer of Adoration

A prayer of adoration is when you praise God for who He is. In this prayer, you tell Him how wonderful, powerful, and loving He is. An example of this prayer is in Psalm 104:1-4:

"Praise the Lord, my soul. Lord my God, you are very great; you are clothed with splendor and majesty. The Lord wraps himself in light as with a garment; he stretches out the heavens like a tent and lays the beams of his upper chambers on their waters..."

Prayer of Confession

1 John 1:8:

"If we claim to be without sin, we deceive ourselves and the truth is not in us."

This is a prayer where you humbly tell God what you've done wrong and ask for His forgiveness. Being honest with God about your mistakes is crucial. 1 John 1:9 says:

"If we confess our sins, he is faithful and just and will forgive us our sins and purify us from all unrighteousness."

God is always ready to forgive you when you come to Him with a genuinely repentant heart.

Prayer of confession.⁹⁷

Prayer of Thanksgiving

In this prayer, thank God for all the good things in your life. Don't focus on what you don't have. Instead, count your blessings and name them one by one, like the Psalmist says. You will see you have more than enough reasons to give thanks to God. 1 Chronicles 16:34, *"Give thanks to the Lord, for he is good; his love endures forever."*

Prayer of Supplication

This is the prayer where you ask for God's help with your needs and the needs of others. You can bring it to God, whether it's something big or small. The Bible says in Ephesians 3:20 that God *"...is able to do immeasurably more than all we ask or imagine, according to his power that is at work within us..."* So, ask him for help.

Suggestions for Integrating Bible Study into Daily Routines

A devotional is a short reading, usually including a Bible verse and a short reflection or story to help you contemplate God's Word. You can read this in the morning with your prayer or any time during the day. It may be brief, but it can set a positive tone for your day and remind you of God's presence.

You can follow a Bible reading plan to guide you on which verses to read each day. Many plans are available online. Some are designed to be read in a year. Others focus on specific topics or books of the Bible. Choose a plan that interests you and fits into your schedule. You can combine your prayer time with Bible study. As you go to God in prayer and Bible study, you will *"... hear a voice behind you, saying, "This is the way; walk in it."* (Isaiah 30:21).

Journaling Prompt

Create a weekly prayer and Bible study schedule. Plan out specific times each day dedicated to prayer and reading the Bible. Use your journal to track your progress, noting insights or answered prayers. Reflect on how this routine strengthens your relationship with God.

Conclusion

As a woman, your life assumes many roles and responsibilities. You may be a mother, a daughter, a sister, a wife, or a friend. Between juggling work, caring for your family, and managing a home, you're usually left feeling overwhelmed. Hence, you need to schedule time for Bible study and prayer. These spiritual tools will help you find peace, guidance, and strength to carry out your daily activities efficiently.

Congratulations on finishing this spiritual journey with this guide. You have invested time and resources in your life and will surely reap the benefits. You discovered how God helped women in the past. You learned about women like Esther, the courageous orphan turned Queen, and Ruth, who was loyal and kind. All the Bible characters featured in this book had moral lessons you could learn from.

Studying the Bible teaches you much about God's love and His will. Studying the Bible and becoming more consistent in prayer connects you with God personally, and you feel His presence enveloping you like a warm blanket. Pray regularly turns you into the lady with a laid-back vibe. You feel and look calmer and less stressed because you know God is listening and everything is working in your favor. The Bible says in Romans 8:28, "And we know that in all things God works for the good of those who love him, who have been called according to his purpose."

Combining Bible study and prayer helps you better decide because when you ask God for guidance, you are confident He will show you the right path. Bible study and prayer help you build stronger relationships. You learn to love and forgive others from Jesus' teaching about God's love and forgiveness. You become more patient and kinder, improving your relationships with your family, friends, and others. You learn to be more understanding and compassionate, seeing others as God sees them.

Finding your divine purpose and direction in life has never been easier. As a woman, you may wonder about your purpose or what you should do with your life. The Bible teaches that God has a plan for everyone, including you. Here's some more good news: You have a guide to refer to whenever you feel lost or confused.

Bible study and consistent prayer are not things you should do. It is something you must do if you wish to excel in all areas of life and fulfill your divine purpose on Earth. Walk with God and watch Him shape you into the glorious queen He created you to be. It is your time to manifest.

Before you close this book, say a prayer with these Bible verses:

- **Psalm 25:4-5:** *"Show me your ways, Lord, teach me your paths. Guide me in your truth and teach me, for you are God my Savior, and my hope is in you all day long."*

- **Psalm 119:35:** *"Direct me in the path of your commands, for there I find delight."*

- **Psalm 86:11:** *"Teach me your way, Lord, that I may rely on your faithfulness; give me an undivided heart, that I may fear your name."*

- **Psalm 19:14:** *"May these words of my mouth and this meditation of my heart be pleasing in your sight, Lord, my Rock, and my Redeemer."*

Part 2: Bible Study Workbook for Women

Grow Closer to God with Guided Reflections, Scripture Prompts, and Weekly Devotionals for Everyday Life

Dedication

To the seekers, the journeyers, and all who long to know God more intimately. May these pages be a humble guide, drawing you closer to the heart of the One who faithfully walks with you every step of the way.

Introduction

Welcome to a year-long journey designed to deepen your understanding of God and empower you to live a life fully aligned with His purposes.

Over the next 52 weeks, we will embark on an intentional exploration of faith, divided into four distinct quarters, each focusing on a vital aspect of our walk with God.

Our path begins by **Knowing God Deeper** (Quarter 1), where we will intimately explore His unchanging attributes and character. From there, we will transition into **Living Out Our Faith** (Quarter 2), delving into the practical ways our beliefs shape our daily actions and choices. The third quarter, **Connecting with Others** (Quarter 3), will guide us in building healthy relationships. Finally, we will conclude with **Living with Purpose** (Quarter 4), discovering and embracing God's unique calling for our lives.

Each week offers a focused theme, relevant Scripture passages for meditation, guided reflection questions, a devotional thought, and a prayer prompt.

Also, each week ends with **a workbook section** where you can document your thoughts and insights.

May this book be a faithful companion, a catalyst for spiritual growth, and a source of profound encouragement as you draw closer to the heart of God.

1. Setting the Foundation (Weeks 1-2)

Week 1: Welcome and Your Journey with God

Take a deep breath.

In the midst of your busy life, you've chosen to carve out this sacred space to connect more deeply with the heart of God. This workbook is a year-long exploration of Scripture, thoughtful reflection, and intentional growth in your relationship with the One who loves you most.

Think of this book as a trusted companion on your faith walk. Each week, we'll gently unpack Biblical truths, ask questions that stir your heart, and offer daily bread for your soul. Our aim is simple yet profound: to help you grow closer to God, not through striving, but through a deeper understanding of His Word and its application to your everyday life.

Your Unique Path

Every woman's journey with God is unique, filled with its own joys, challenges, and moments of profound connection. Whether you've walked with Him for many years or are just beginning to explore His love, this workbook welcomes you exactly where you are. There's no expectation of perfection, only an invitation to be open and honest with yourself and with God.

Take a moment now to quiet your heart and consider:

What has your journey with God looked like so far?

_____

_____

_____

What are some significant moments or experiences that come to mind?

_____

_____

_____

What are your deepest longings for your relationship with God right now?

_____

_____

_____

What does "growing closer" look and feel like to you?

_____

_____

_____

What hopes do you have as you begin this year-long study?

_____

_____

_____

Scripture Prompt:

Spend some time meditating on **Psalm 139:23-24**:

"Search me, O God, and know my heart! Try me and know my thoughts! And see if there be any grievous way in me, and lead me in the way everlasting!" (ESV))

What words or phrases in this psalm resonate with you today?

_____

_____

_____

What does it mean for God to search your heart?

_____

_____

_____

How does this desire for God's searching relate to your own desire to grow closer to Him?

_____

_____

_____

Guided Reflection:

Use a notebook to jot down your thoughts and responses to the questions we unpacked and your reflections on Psalm 139:23-24. Be honest and allow yourself to be vulnerable. This is a conversation between you and God.

Weekly Devotional: The Importance of Consistent Connection

Finding consistent time for what truly matters can feel like a constant battle. Yet, just as regular nourishment sustains our physical bodies, consistent connection with God through His Word and prayer nourishes our souls. It's in these intentional moments that we learn to recognize His voice, understand His character, and experience the depth of His love.

This weekly devotional, along with the daily Scripture readings and reflection prompts, is designed to be a gentle rhythm in your week. It's about creating space for your spirit to breathe and be filled.

As you commit to this year-long journey, remember that even small, consistent steps can lead to growth. Be patient with yourself, celebrate the small victories, and trust that God will meet you in the quiet moments of study and reflection.

Prayer Prompt:

Take a few moments to pray about your journey ahead. Ask God to open your heart and mind to His Word, to reveal Himself to you in new ways, and to guide you as you seek to grow closer to Him.

Personal Reflection & Growth Journal

Significant Moments / Insights from This Week's Study

What happened? What was the insight?

_____

_____

_____

_____

_____

Emotional/Spiritual Responses:

_____

_____

_____

_____

_____

Spiritual Insights/Lessons Learned:

- First thoughts:

_____

_____

_____

_____

- New perspectives gained:

_____

_____

_____

_____

- My Response/Action:

_____

_____

_____

_____

What helped me connect with God/grow this ?week?

_____

_____

_____

_____

What hindered my connection/?growth?

_____

_____

_____

_____

Week 2: The Power and Purpose of God's Word

Stepping into Scripture

Last week, we began by acknowledging our individual journeys and our desire for deeper connection with God. This week, we turn our attention to the very tool God has given us to know Him intimately: His Word, the Bible.

The Bible is living and active (Hebrews 4:12), a divine tapestry woven with threads of history, poetry, prophecy, and personal encounters with God. It reveals His character, His promises, His plan for humanity, and His unfailing love for you.

Think about your current relationship with the Bible:

- How often do you engage with Scripture? What does that engagement typically look like?
- What are some of your perceptions or feelings about reading the Bible? Do you find it encouraging, challenging, confusing, comforting?
- What do you hope to gain from studying the Bible more intentionally this year?

Scripture Prompt:

Reflect on **2 Timothy 3:16-17**:

"All Scripture is breathed out by God and profitable for teaching, for reproof, for correction, and for training in righteousness, that the man of God may be complete, equipped for every good work."(ESV))

What does it mean to you that Scripture is "breathed out by God"? What are the different ways this passage says Scripture is "profitable"? How does engaging with Scripture equip you for "every good work?"

Guided Reflection:

Use your notebook to record your thoughts on the questions above and your reflections on 2 Timothy 3:16-17. Consider any past experiences with Scripture that have been particularly meaningful or challenging.

Weekly Devotional: Engaging with Scripture for Transformation

Simply reading the Bible is a good start, but true growth comes when we engage with it actively and intentionally. This means not just reading words but seeking to understand their meaning within their historical and literary context, reflecting on how they apply to our lives, and allowing them to shape our thoughts, attitudes, and actions.

Throughout this workbook, you'll be encouraged to go beyond surface-level reading through the daily prompts and weekly reflections. These are designed to help you:

- **Understand:** What does this passage truly mean?

- **Reflect:** How does this truth relate to my life and experiences?

- **Apply:** What practical steps can I take based on what I've learned?

This active engagement is key to transformation. As we consistently immerse ourselves in God's Word and allow it to speak to our hearts, we will indeed grow closer to Him and become more equipped for the life He has called us to live.

Prayer Prompt:

Pray that God would give you a hunger for His Word and the wisdom to understand it. Ask Him to open your eyes to the truths He wants to reveal to you this year and to help you apply them to your daily life.

Personal Reflection & Growth Journal

Significant Moments / Insights from This Week's Study

What happened? What was the insight?

_____

_____

_____

_____

Emotional/Spiritual Responses:

_____

_____

_____

_____

Spiritual Insights/Lessons Learned:

- First thoughts:

_____

_____

_____

_____

- New perspectives gained:

_____

_____

_____

_____

- My Response/Action:

_____

_____

_____

_____

What helped me connect with God/grow this ?week?

_____

_____

_____

_____

What hindered my connection/?growth?

_____

_____

_____

_____

I. Quarter 1: Knowing God Deeper (Weeks 3-15) - Theme: Exploring God's Attributes

Week 3: God Our Creator

Let's start at the very beginning, focusing on God as our Creator. The opening words of Scripture start with, "In the beginning, God..." (Genesis 1:1). This foundational truth shapes everything we understand about ourselves, our world, and our relationship with Him.

Think for a moment about the sheer wonder of creation. From the smallest seed that bursts forth with life to the vast expanse of the cosmos, everything bears the imprint of God's power, wisdom, and artistry.

Consider these aspects of God as Creator:

- What comes to mind when you think about God creating the universe? What emotions or thoughts does it evoke?
- In what ways do you see God's creativity reflected in the world around you today? Consider both the grand scale and the intricate details.
- How does the knowledge that God created you personally (Psalm 139:13-16) impact how you view yourself?

Scripture Prompt:

Meditate on **Genesis 1:1**:

> *"In the beginning, God created the heavens and the earth."*
> (ESV)

What is the significance of the very first words of the Bible? What does this statement tell us about God's priority and power? How does this foundational truth influence your understanding of everything else in Scripture?

Now, also read **Psalm 19:1**:

> *"The heavens declare the glory of God, and the sky above proclaims his handiwork."* (ESV))

How does the natural world serve as a testament to God's glory? What aspects of creation specifically point to His "handiwork"?

Guided Reflection:

Use a notebook or journal to record your reflections on the questions above and your insights from Genesis 1:1 and Psalm 19:1. Pay attention to any new perspectives or deeper understandings that emerge as you ponder God's role as Creator.

Weekly Devotional: Finding God in the Created World

Sometimes, in our pursuit of God, we focus solely on the written Word or specific spiritual practices. While these are vital, we can also encounter God in the beauty and order of the world He has made. The intricate patterns of a flower, the breathtaking vista of a mountain range, the delicate balance of an ecosystem all whisper of His power and design.

Taking time to observe creation can be an act of worship.

It allows us to see glimpses of God's character: His creativity, His attention to detail, His boundless power, and His inherent beauty. As you go about your week, try to be more intentional about noticing the wonders around you. In these moments, you can connect with the Creator through His creation.

Prayer Prompt:

Spend time in prayer thanking God for His creation. Ask Him to open your eyes to see His handiwork in new ways and to deepen your appreciation for His power and artistry.

Personal Reflection & Growth Journal

Significant Moments / Insights from This Week's Study

What happened? What was the insight?

_____

_____

_____

_____

_____

Emotional/Spiritual Responses:

_____

_____

_____

_____

Spiritual Insights/Lessons Learned:

- First thoughts:

_____

_____

_____

- New perspectives gained:

_____

_____

_____

- My Response/Action:

_____

_____

_____

_____

What helped me connect with God/grow this ?week?

_____

_____

_____

_____

What hindered my connection/?growth?

_____

_____

_____

_____

Week 4: God's Unfailing Love

We now turn to one of the most comforting and foundational truths about our Heavenly Creator: His unfailing love. This isn't a fleeting emotion or a conditional affection; it is a deep, steadfast, and unwavering commitment to us.

Think about the times in your life when you have felt deeply loved. What did that feel like? Now, try to grasp the magnitude of a love that is even greater, a love that never gives up, never fails, and is offered freely and abundantly by the Creator of the universe.

Reflect on these aspects of God's unfailing love:

- How does the idea of God's unfailing love differ from human love that can sometimes waver or end? What comfort does this bring you?

- Can you recall a time when you particularly felt God's love for you? What circumstances surrounded that experience?

- How does understanding God's love impact the way you view yourself and your worth?

Scripture Prompt:

Spend time meditating on **Romans 5:8**:

> *"but God shows his love for us in that while we were still sinners, Christ died for us."* (ESV)

What does it mean that God showed His love for us *while we were still sinners*? What does this reveal about the nature of His love? How does the sacrifice of Christ demonstrate the depth of this love?

Now, also read **1 John 4:8**:

> *"Anyone who does not love does not know God, because God is love."* (ESV)

How does this verse define God's very essence? What does it imply about everything He does? How should this understanding shape our own capacity for love?

Guided Reflection:

Use a notebook or your journal to record your reflections on the questions above and your insights from Romans 5:8 and 1 John 4:8. Allow yourself to truly absorb the profound truth of God's love for you.

Weekly Devotional: Resting in God's Affection

In a world that often demands performance and measures worth by achievement, the unconditional love of God stands as a powerful anchor. We don't have to earn it, strive for it, or be perfect to receive it. It is freely given, a gift born out of His very nature.

This week, focus on resting in God's love. Take moments throughout your day to remind yourself that you are deeply loved by the Creator of the universe. Allow this truth to wash over you, bringing comfort, security, and a sense of belonging.

Consider how this unfailing love can transform the way you interact with yourself and others. When we are secure in God's love, we are freer to extend grace, forgive imperfections (both our own and others'), and live with a greater sense of peace and joy.

Prayer Prompt:

Spend time in prayer thanking God for His unfailing love. Ask Him to help you truly grasp the depth and breadth of His affection for you and to empower you to live in the light of that love.

Personal Reflection & Growth Journal

Significant Moments / Insights from This Week's Study

What happened? What was the insight?

_____

_____

_____

_____

_____

Emotional/Spiritual Responses:

_____

_____

_____

_____

Spiritual Insights/Lessons Learned:

- First thoughts:

_____

_____

_____

- New perspectives gained:

_____

_____

_____

- My Response/Action:

_____

_____

_____

_____

What helped me connect with God/grow this ?week?

_____

_____

_____

_____

What hindered my connection/?growth?

_____

_____

_____

_____

Week 5: God's Perfect Holiness

After reflecting on God's love, we now turn to another crucial aspect of His character: His perfect holiness. While His love draws us near, His holiness reminds us of His complete otherness, His absolute purity, and His separation from all that is sinful or imperfect. Understanding God's holiness helps us grasp the depth of His righteousness and the seriousness of sin.

Take a moment to consider what the word "holy" means to you. What images or ideas come to mind? It's more than just being "good"; it speaks of a complete and utter perfection, a moral purity beyond our full comprehension.

Reflect on these aspects of God's perfect holiness:

- How does the concept of God's holiness make you feel? Does it inspire awe, reverence, or perhaps even a sense of distance? Why?

- In what ways does God's holiness contrast with the imperfections and sinfulness we see in the world and in ourselves?

- How does understanding God's holiness deepen your appreciation for His grace and mercy?

Scripture Prompt:

Spend time meditating on **Leviticus 19:2**:

"You shall be holy, for I the Lord your God am holy." (ESV))

What does it mean that God commands us to be holy because He is holy? Is this a call to perfection? How can we, as imperfect beings, strive for holiness?

Now, also read **Isaiah 6:3**:

"And one called to another and said: 'Holy, holy, holy is the Lord of hosts; the whole earth is full of his glory!'" (ESV))

What is the significance of the repetition of "holy" three times? What does it emphasize about God's character? How does the vision of God's holiness in this passage impact your understanding of His majesty?

Guided Reflection:

Use your notebook or journal to record your reflections on the questions above and your insights from Leviticus 19:2 and Isaiah 6:3. Be honest about any challenges or questions you have regarding God's holiness.

Weekly Devotional: Approaching a Holy God

The perfect holiness of God can sometimes feel intimidating. How can we, with our flaws and failings, draw near to someone so utterly pure? The answer lies in God's own provision: through the sacrifice of Jesus Christ, we are made righteous in His sight. It is through His Son that we can approach the holy God with confidence and without fear of condemnation.

Understanding God's holiness should not drive us away but rather inspire a deeper reverence and a greater appreciation for the gift of grace. It reminds us of the seriousness of sin and the immense cost of our redemption. As we grow in our understanding of God's holiness, may it lead us to a greater desire for purity in our own lives, not out of obligation, but out of a longing to honor the One who is altogether holy.

Prayer Prompt:

Spend time in prayer acknowledging God's perfect holiness. Thank Him for the way He has made it possible for you to draw near to Him through Christ. Ask for His help in growing in holiness in your own life, reflecting His purity in your thoughts, words, and actions.

Personal Reflection & Growth Journal

Significant Moments / Insights from This Week's Study

What happened? What was the insight?

_____

_____

_____

_____

_____

Emotional/Spiritual Responses:

_____

_____

_____

_____

Spiritual Insights/Lessons Learned:

• First thoughts:

_____

_____

_____

• New perspectives gained:

_____

_____

_____

- My Response/Action:

_____

_____

_____

_____

What helped me connect with God/grow this ?week?

_____

_____

_____

_____

What hindered my connection/?growth?

_____

_____

_____

_____

Week 6: God's Abundant Grace

Having contemplated God's perfect holiness, we now turn to His abundant grace. Grace is often defined as God's unmerited favor: His loving-kindness and mercy freely given, not because we deserve it, but because of His generous nature. It is the very essence of how He interacts with us, especially considering our imperfections.

Think about times in your life when you received unexpected kindness or help. How did that make you feel? God's grace is infinitely more profound, a constant outpouring of His goodness towards us.

Reflect on these aspects of God's abundant grace:

- What does the phrase "unmerited favor" truly mean to you in the context of your relationship with God?
- Can you identify specific instances in your life where you have experienced God's grace, even when you felt undeserving?
- How does understanding God's grace free you from feelings of guilt, shame, or the need to constantly earn His approval?

Scripture Prompt:

Spend time meditating on **Ephesians 2:8-9**:

"For by grace you have been saved through faith. And this is not your own doing; it is the gift of God, not a result of works, so that no one may boast." (ESV))

What does this passage tell us about how salvation is received? What role does grace play? Why is it emphasized that salvation is "not your own doing" or "a result of works"?

Now, also read **Titus 3:5**:

"he saved us, not because of works done by us in righteousness, but according to his own mercy, by the washing of regeneration and renewal of the Holy Spirit," (ESV)

How does this verse further emphasize that our salvation is based on God's mercy rather than our own good deeds? What is the significance of "regeneration and renewal of the Holy Spirit" in the context of His grace?

Guided Reflection:

Use your notebook or journal to record your reflections on the questions above and your insights from Ephesians 2:8-9 and Titus 3:5. Consider how the truth of God's grace impacts your understanding of your worth and your relationship with Him.

Weekly Devotional: Living in the Light of Grace

The abundant grace of God is not just a one-time gift at the moment of salvation; it is the very atmosphere in which we live as believers. It fuels our growth, forgives our failures, and empowers us to live in a way that honors Him.

When we truly understand and embrace God's grace, it transforms our perspective. We move from a place of striving and fear to a place of rest and confidence in His love. We become more willing to extend grace to others, knowing how freely it has been given to us.

This week, let's consciously choose to live in the light of God's grace. Release any burdens of guilt or the need for self-justification. Embrace the freedom that comes from knowing you are loved and accepted, not because of what you've done, but because of who God is.

Prayer Prompt:

Spend time in prayer thanking God for His abundant grace. Ask Him to help you fully receive and live in the reality of His unmerited favor. Pray for the ability to extend that same grace to those around you.

Personal Reflection & Growth Journal

Significant Moments / Insights from This Week's Study

What happened? What was the insight?

_____

_____

_____

_____

Emotional/Spiritual Responses:

_____

_____

_____

_____

Spiritual Insights/Lessons Learned:

- First thoughts:

_____

_____

_____

_____

- New perspectives gained:

_____

_____

_____

_____

- My Response/Action:

_____

_____

_____

_____

What helped me connect with God/grow this ?week?

_____

_____

_____

_____

What hindered my connection/?growth?

_____

_____

_____

_____

Week 7: God's Unchanging Faithfulness

The unchanging faithfulness of God provides a solid anchor for our souls. His promises are true, His love endures, and His commitment to us never wavers, regardless of our circumstances or feelings. This steadfastness is a cornerstone of our trust in Him.

Think about the things in your life that have been unreliable or have let you down. Now, contrast that with the character of God, who is consistently true to His Word and His nature.

Reflect on these aspects of God's unchanging faithfulness:

- What does it mean to you that God's faithfulness is *unchanging*? How does this provide security and hope in your life?

- Can you recall a time when you experienced God's faithfulness in a tangible way, perhaps during a difficult season?

- How does knowing that God is always faithful impact your own commitment and loyalty in your relationships and to Him?

Scripture Prompt:

Spend time meditating on **Lamentations 3:22-23**:

"The steadfast love of the Lord never ceases; his mercies never come to an end; they are new every morning; great is your faithfulness." (ESV)

What does this passage emphasize about the consistency and renewal of God's love and mercies? What does it mean that His faithfulness is "great" and "new every morning"? How can this truth sustain you through challenging times?

Now, also read **Hebrews 13:8**:

"Jesus Christ is the same yesterday and today and forever." (ESV)

How does the unchanging nature of Jesus Christ reflect the unchanging faithfulness of God? What comfort do you find in this constant presence and character of Christ?

Guided Reflection:

Use your notebook or journal to record your reflections on the questions above and your insights from Lamentations 3:22-23 and Hebrews 13:8. Consider specific areas of your life where you need to rely on God's unwavering faithfulness.

Weekly Devotional: Trusting in God's Promises

Because God is unchangingly faithful, we can have complete confidence in His promises. Throughout Scripture, He has declared His love, His provision, His guidance, and His eternal presence with us. When life feels uncertain and the ground beneath us seems to shift, we can stand firm on the solid rock of His Word.

This week let's focus on identifying and claiming God's promises for our lives. As you read Scripture, pay attention to the declarations He makes about His character and His intentions toward His children.

Remind yourself that He is not a God who lies or changes His mind (Numbers 23:19). His faithfulness extends to every generation.

By anchoring ourselves in God's promises, we cultivate a deeper trust and resilience in the face of life's storms. We learn to lean not on our own understanding or fleeting circumstances, but on the One whose faithfulness endures forever.

Prayer Prompt:

Spend time in prayer thanking God for His unchanging faithfulness. Ask Him to bring specific promises from His Word to your mind and heart. Pray for the grace to trust in these promises, especially when circumstances seem contrary.

Personal Reflection & Growth Journal

Significant Moments / Insights from This Week's Study

What happened? What was the insight?

_____

_____

_____

_____

_____

Emotional/Spiritual Responses:

_____

_____

_____

_____

_____

Spiritual Insights/Lessons Learned:
  • First thoughts:

_____

_____

_____

- New perspectives gained:

_____

_____

_____

_____

- My Response/Action:

_____

_____

_____

_____

What helped me connect with God/grow this ?week?

_____

_____

_____

_____

What hindered my connection/?growth?

_____

_____

_____

_____

Week 8: God's All-Knowing Wisdom

Life often presents us with complex situations, difficult decisions, and paths that aren't always clear. Yet, we serve a God whose understanding is infinite, whose wisdom encompasses all things. He sees the beginning from the end, knows every detail, and possesses perfect insight into every circumstance. This all-knowing wisdom is a profound comfort and a guide for our lives.

Consider the times you've sought guidance or understanding. Reflect on the limitations of human knowledge and the peace that comes from trusting a source of perfect wisdom.

Reflect on these aspects of God's all-knowing wisdom:

- How does the knowledge that God knows everything about you – your thoughts, your past, your future – make you feel? Does it bring comfort or unease? Why?

- Can you recall a time when you sought God's wisdom in a challenging situation? How did He guide you?

- How does trusting in God's wisdom differ from relying solely on your own understanding or the advice of others?

Scripture Prompt:

Spend time meditating on **Proverbs 3:5-6**:

"Trust in the Lord with all your heart, and do not lean on your own understanding. In all your ways acknowledge him, and he will make straight your paths." (ESV)

What does it mean to "not lean on your own understanding"? What does it look like to "acknowledge him in all your ways"? What is the promise that follows this trust and acknowledgement?

Now, also read **Romans 11:33**:

"Oh, the depth of the riches and wisdom and knowledge of God! How unsearchable are his judgments and how inscrutable his ways!" (ESV)

What does this exclamation convey about the extent of God's wisdom and knowledge? How does the idea that His judgments are "unsearchable" and His ways "inscrutable" impact your perspective on trying to fully understand God?

Guided Reflection:

Use your notebook or journal to write down your reflections on the questions above and your insights from Proverbs 3:5-6 and Romans 11:33. Consider areas in your life where you need to release your own understanding and trust in God's wisdom.

Weekly Devotional: Leaning on Divine Understanding

Human wisdom is limited and often influenced by our emotions, experiences, and biases. God's wisdom, however, is pure, objective, and sees the complete picture. When we face decisions or uncertainties, seeking His perspective through prayer and His Word offers guidance that surpasses our own understanding.

This week let's practice intentionally seeking God's wisdom in our daily lives. Before making a decision, big or small, take a moment to pray and ask for His guidance. As you read Scripture, look for principles and truths that can illuminate your path. Remember that trusting in God's wisdom doesn't always mean we'll understand everything, but it does mean we can have confidence that His way is best.

Cultivating a posture of humility, acknowledging our limitations, and consistently turning to God for insight will deepen our reliance on His all-knowing mind and lead us on paths that are ultimately for our good and His glory.

Prayer Prompt:

Spend time in prayer asking God for His wisdom and discernment in specific areas of your life where you need guidance. Pray for a humble heart that is willing to follow His leading, even when it doesn't align with your own initial thoughts.

Personal Reflection & Growth Journal

Significant Moments / Insights from This Week's Study

What happened? What was the insight?

_____

_____

_____

_____

_____

Emotional/Spiritual Responses:

_____

_____

_____

_____

Spiritual Insights/Lessons Learned:
- First thoughts:

_____

_____

_____

_____

- New perspectives gained:

_____

_____

_____

_____

- My Response/Action:

_____

_____

_____

_____

What helped me connect with God/grow this ?week?

_____

_____

_____

_____

What hindered my connection/?growth?

_____

_____

_____

_____

Week 9: God's Everywhere Presence

We navigate days filled with various locations, tasks, and interactions. Yet, one constant remains for the believer: the unwavering presence of God. Scripture assures us that He is not distant or confined but is with us wherever we go. This truth of God's omnipresence offers immense comfort and security.

Consider moments when you have felt alone or isolated. Reflect on the reassurance that comes from knowing God is always near, even when unseen.

Reflect on these aspects of God's everywhere presence:

- How does the understanding that God is always with you impact your feelings of loneliness or fear?
- In what everyday situations can you consciously recognize God's presence around you?
- How does the knowledge of God's omnipresence influence the way you behave and make choices, knowing He is always aware?

Scripture Prompt:

Spend time meditating on **Psalm 139:7-12**:

> *"Where shall I go from your Spirit? Or where shall I flee from your presence? If I ascend to heaven, you are there! If I make my bed in Sheol, you are there! If I take the wings of the morning and dwell in the uttermost parts of the sea, even there your hand shall lead me, and your right hand shall hold me fast. If I say, "Surely the darkness shall cover me, and the light about me be night," even the darkness is not dark to you; the night is bright as the day, for darkness is as light with you."* (ESV)

What feelings or thoughts arise as you read this powerful description of God's omnipresence? What comfort do you find in the truth that there is nowhere you can go to escape His presence? How does the imagery of darkness and light relate to His awareness of you?

Now, also read **Acts 17:28**:

> *"for 'In him we live and move and have our being'; as even some of your own poets have said, 'For we are indeed his offspring.'"* (ESV)

What does it mean to live, move, and have our being "in him"? How does this verse emphasize the intimate and constant connection we have with God?

Guided Reflection:

Use your notebook or journal to record your reflections on the questions above and your insights from Psalm 139:7-12 and Acts 17:28. Consider specific times and places where you can intentionally acknowledge God's nearness this week.

Weekly Devotional: Walking with God Throughout the Day

The reality of God's omnipresence transforms our daily routines. Knowing He is always near means we never truly face any moment alone. Whether we are at work, with family, running errands, or in quiet solitude, His presence surrounds us, offering comfort, guidance, and companionship.

This week let's cultivate an awareness of God's nearness in the ordinary moments of our days. Speak to Him as you go about your tasks. Acknowledge His presence in the beauty you see, the challenges you face, and the interactions you have. Remember that prayer is not confined to specific times or places; it can be a continuous conversation with the God who is always with you.

By consciously recognizing His omnipresence, we move from simply believing He is everywhere to experiencing His nearness in a tangible way. This awareness fosters a deeper sense of connection and allows us to walk through each day with the constant assurance of His love and support.

Prayer Prompt:

Spend time in prayer thanking God for His constant presence in your life. Ask for a greater awareness of His nearness throughout your day and for the comfort and guidance that comes from knowing He is always with you.

Personal Reflection & Growth Journal

Significant Moments / Insights from This Week's Study

What happened? What was the insight?

_____

_____

_____

_____

Emotional/Spiritual Responses:

_____

_____

_____

_____

Spiritual Insights/Lessons Learned:

- First thoughts:

_____

_____

_____

_____

- New perspectives gained:

_____

_____

_____

_____

- My Response/Action:

_____

_____

_____

_____

What helped me connect with God/grow this ?week?

_____

_____

_____

_____

What hindered my connection/?growth?

_____

_____

_____

_____

Week 10: God's Ultimate Power

As we continue to explore the depths of God's character, we encounter His ultimate power. He is not limited or constrained; His strength and authority are absolute. He spoke the universe into existence, and His power sustains all things. Understanding this attribute brings us a sense of security and hope, knowing that nothing is beyond His control.

Consider situations in your life that feel overwhelming or impossible. Reflect on the comfort that comes from knowing there is a God whose power surpasses all limitations.

Reflect on these aspects of God's ultimate power:

- When you think about God's power, what images or events from Scripture come to mind? (e.g., creation, miracles, resurrection)
- How does knowing that God has ultimate power impact your fears and anxieties?
- In what areas of your life do you need to trust more fully in God's power to work?

Scripture Prompt:

Spend time meditating on **Psalm 62:11**:

> *"Once God has spoken; twice have I heard this: that power belongs to God,"* (ESV)

What is the significance of the repetition in this verse? What is the clear declaration being made about power? How does this singular truth shape your understanding of the world and your place in it?

Now, also read **Matthew 19:26**:

> *"But Jesus looked at them and said, "With man this is impossible, but with God all things are possible.""* (ESV)

In what context was Jesus speaking these words? How does this statement about God's possibility relate to the challenges you face? What does it mean to live with the understanding that "all things are possible" with God?

Guided Reflection:

Use your notebook or journal to write down your reflections on the questions above and your insights from Psalm 62:11 and Matthew 19:26. Consider specific challenges you are facing and how trusting in God's ultimate power can shift your perspective.

Weekly Devotional: Relying on God's Strength

Our own strength and resources are often limited. We encounter obstacles that seem insurmountable and face situations where we feel powerless. It is in these moments that the reality of God's ultimate power becomes our greatest hope. He is not only capable but willing to intervene and work on our behalf.

This week let's consciously choose to rely on God's strength rather than our own. Bring your weaknesses and limitations before Him, trusting that His power is made perfect in our weakness (2 Corinthians 12:9). Remember that the same power that raised Jesus from the dead is available to those who believe.

By acknowledging our need for His strength and actively seeking His help, we open ourselves to experience His power in tangible ways. This doesn't always mean our circumstances will change as we desire, but it does mean we can face them with a supernatural strength and a confident hope in the One who holds all power in His hands.

Prayer Prompt:

Spend time in prayer acknowledging God's ultimate power and sovereignty. Bring before Him any situations where you feel powerless or overwhelmed. Ask for His strength to sustain you and His power to work in and through those circumstances.

Personal Reflection & Growth Journal

Significant Moments / Insights from This Week's Study

What happened? What was the insight?

_____

_____

_____

_____

_____

Emotional/Spiritual Responses:

_____

_____

_____

_____

_____

Spiritual Insights/Lessons Learned:

- First thoughts:

_____

_____

_____

_____

- New perspectives gained:

_____

_____

_____

_____

- My Response/Action:

_____

_____

_____

_____

What helped me connect with God/grow this ?week?

_____

_____

_____

_____

What hindered my connection/?growth?

_____

_____

_____

_____

Week 11: God's Perfect Justice

We live in a world where injustice often prevails, where the innocent suffer and the guilty sometimes go unpunished. In contrast to this, God's perfect justice is a comforting assurance. He is righteous and fair in all His judgments. His justice is not driven by emotion or bias but by His perfect understanding of truth and righteousness.

Consider times you have witnessed or experienced injustice. Reflect on the longing for true fairness and the comfort that God's perfect justice offers.

Reflect on these aspects of God's perfect justice:

- How does the knowledge of God's perfect justice bring you comfort in a world filled with unfairness?

- In what ways does God's justice differ from human justice systems? What are the limitations of human judgment?

- How does understanding God's justice influence your own approach to fairness and your response to injustice around you?

Scripture Prompt:

Spend time meditating on **Psalm 89:14**:

"Righteousness and justice are the foundation of your throne; steadfast love and faithfulness go before you." (ESV)

What does it mean that righteousness and justice are the "foundation" of God's throne? How do His steadfast love and faithfulness relate to His justice? What does this tell you about the nature of God's rule?

Now, also read **Romans 12:19**:

"Beloved, never avenge yourselves, but leave it to the wrath of God, for it is written, "Vengeance is mine, I will repay, says the Lord."" (ESV)

Why are we instructed not to seek our own revenge? What does this passage reveal about God's role in administering justice? How does trusting in His justice bring freedom from bitterness and the need for personal retribution?

Guided Reflection:

Write down your reflections on the questions above and your insights from Psalm 89:14 and Romans 12:19. Consider any situations where you need to release the desire for personal vengeance and trust in God's perfect justice.

Weekly Devotional: Trusting in God's Righteousness

Because God's justice is perfect, we can trust that ultimately, all things will be made right. This doesn't always mean we will see justice unfold according to our timing or understanding, but it assures us that God's righteousness will prevail. He sees every wrong, knows every motive, and will ultimately judge with perfect fairness.

This week let's focus on cultivating a deep trust in God's righteousness. When we witness or experience injustice, let us remember that He is the ultimate judge. This doesn't excuse us from seeking justice in our own spheres of influence, but it frees us from the burden of carrying anger and resentment.

By trusting in God's perfect justice, we can find peace knowing that He is in control and that His way is ultimately right. We can release the need for immediate resolution and rest in the assurance that His justice will prevail in His perfect time.

Prayer Prompt:

Spend time in prayer acknowledging God's perfect justice and righteousness. Bring before Him any situations where you long for justice. Ask for His peace and the ability to trust in His timing and His ways. Pray for wisdom in how to respond to injustice in a way that honors Him.

Personal Reflection & Growth Journal

Significant Moments / Insights from This Week's Study

What happened? What was the insight?

_____

_____

_____

_____

_____

Emotional/Spiritual Responses:

_____

_____

_____

_____

Spiritual Insights/Lessons Learned:
  • First thoughts:

_____

_____

_____

- New perspectives gained:

_____

_____

_____

_____

- My Response/Action:

_____

_____

_____

_____

What helped me connect with God/grow this ?week?

_____

_____

_____

_____

What hindered my connection/?growth?

_____

_____

_____

_____

Week 12: God's Tender Mercy

While God's holiness reveals the seriousness of sin and His justice ensures fairness, His tender mercy is the compassionate outpouring of His love towards those who are hurting, broken, and in need. It is His willingness to forgive, to comfort, and to extend grace in the face of our failures and weaknesses.

Think about times when you have needed compassion or forgiveness. Reflect on the relief and comfort that mercy brings. God's mercy is far greater and more tender than any we can imagine.

Reflect on these aspects of God's tender mercy:

- How does the idea of God's tender mercy resonate with your own experiences of needing forgiveness or comfort?
- In what ways do you see God's mercy extended in the world around you, both in your own life and in the lives of others?
- How does receiving God's tender mercy influence your ability to show mercy and compassion to those around you?

Scripture Prompt:

Spend time meditating on **Psalm 103:8**:

"The Lord is merciful and gracious, slow to anger and abounding in steadfast love." (ESV)

What do the words "merciful" and "gracious" convey about God's character in this verse? What does it mean that He is "slow to anger" and "abounding in steadfast love"? How does this description offer you comfort and assurance?

Now, also read **Ephesians 2:4-5**:

"But God, being rich in mercy, because of the great love with which he loved us, even when we were dead in our trespasses, made us alive together with Christ—by grace you have been saved" (ESV)

What does it mean that God is "rich in mercy"? How did His mercy manifest itself towards us "even when we were dead in our trespasses"? How does this connect with the concept of salvation by grace?

Guided Reflection:

Write down your answers on the questions above and your insights from Psalm 103:8 and Ephesians 2:4-5. Consider specific areas where you need to receive God's tender mercy or extend it to others.

Weekly Devotional: Receiving and Giving Mercy

God's tender mercy is a gift freely given, and as recipients of this grace, we are called to extend the same compassion to those around us. Just as He meets us in our brokenness with understanding and forgiveness, we are to approach others with gentleness and empathy.

This week let's be intentional about both receiving and giving mercy. Allow yourself to be embraced by God's tender care, acknowledging your own need for His grace. At the same time, look for opportunities to show compassion to those who are struggling, offering a listening ear, a helping hand, or a word of encouragement.

By embracing God's mercy and extending it to others, we reflect His character and become instruments of His love in the world. This reciprocal flow of mercy fosters healing, understanding, and deeper connection within our communities and with God.

Prayer Prompt:

Spend time in prayer thanking God for His tender mercy in your life. Ask for a greater awareness of His compassion and for a heart that is more readily able to extend that same mercy to others, especially those who may be difficult to love or forgive.

Personal Reflection & Growth Journal

Significant Moments / Insights from This Week's Study

What happened? What was the insight?

_____

_____

_____

_____

_____

Emotional/Spiritual Responses:

_____

_____

_____

_____

Spiritual Insights/Lessons Learned:

- First thoughts:

_____

_____

_____

_____

- New perspectives gained:

_____

_____

_____

_____

- My Response/Action:

_____

_____

_____

_____

What helped me connect with God/grow this ?week?

_____

_____

_____

_____

What hindered my connection/?growth?

_____

_____

_____

_____

Week 13: Review and Reflection on Knowing God

The Lord is
my shepherd;
I shall not want.

PSALM 23:1

We've journeyed through a rich landscape of God's character over the past eleven weeks, exploring His roles as Creator, His unfailing love, perfect holiness, abundant grace, unchanging faithfulness, all-knowing wisdom, everywhere presence, ultimate power, perfect justice, and tender mercy. This week is set aside to pause, reflect, and allow these truths to settle more deeply into our hearts.

Think back over the attributes we've studied. What has resonated with you most? What challenged your understanding? How has your perception of God grown or shifted during this time?

Scripture Prompt:

Spend time meditating on **James 4:8:**

"Draw near to God, and he will draw near to you."(ESV)

In what ways have you felt God drawing near to you as you've studied His attributes? What steps can you take to continue drawing near to Him?

Guided Reflection:

Reflect on the attributes of God explored in Weeks 3 through 12. Consider the following questions:

- Which attribute of God surprised you the most or gave you a new perspective?

- How has understanding God's [choose one or two specific attributes] impacted your daily life or your relationship with Him?

- What is one thing you want to remember or apply from this quarter's study of God's character?

- In what ways do you sense a desire to know God even more deeply as a result of this study?

Devotional: Continuing to Seek Deeper Knowledge of God

Our exploration of God's attributes this quarter is not an endpoint but rather a step further on a lifelong journey of knowing Him. The more we learn about who He is, the more we understand His love for us and His purposes for our lives.

Continue to cultivate a curiosity about God. Remain open to learning and growing in your understanding of His multifaceted character. Engage with Scripture with a desire to see Him more clearly. Talk to Him in prayer about what you are learning and how it impacts you.

The desire to know God more intimately is a holy pursuit. May the insights gained in these past weeks fuel a continued passion to seek His face and to grow in your relationship with the One who is all-encompassing and eternally worthy of our adoration.

Prayer Prompt:

Spend time in prayer thanking God for revealing more of Himself to you during this quarter. Ask for a continued hunger to know Him more deeply and for His guidance as you continue your study in the weeks ahead.

Personal Reflection & Growth Journal

Significant Moments / Insights from This Week's Study

What happened? What was the insight?

_____

_____

_____

_____

_____

Emotional/Spiritual Responses:

_____

_____

_____

_____

_____

Spiritual Insights/Lessons Learned:

- First thoughts:

_____

_____

_____

_____

- New perspectives gained:

_____

_____

_____

_____

- My Response/Action:

_____

_____

_____

_____

What helped me connect with God/grow this ?week?

_____

_____

_____

_____

What hindered my connection/?growth?

_____

_____

_____

_____

Week 14: From Knowing to Living: Bridging Understanding and Action

The foundation we've laid in understanding who God is will now inform how we live out our faith in the everyday rhythms of our lives.

Think about how a deeper understanding of God's love, grace, and faithfulness, for example, might influence your interactions with others or your approach to challenges. The knowledge we've gained is not meant to remain abstract; it is intended to shape our actions and attitudes.

Scripture Prompt:

Spend time meditating on **Philippians 3:10**:

> *"that I may know him and the power of his resurrection, and may share his sufferings, becoming like him in his death,"* (ESV)

Notice Paul's desire here. It goes beyond intellectual knowledge to a deeper, experiential knowing of Christ, including the power of His resurrection and even a sharing in His sufferings. How does this verse challenge your own pursuit of knowing God? How might a deeper knowing of Him empower you to live differently?

Guided Reflection:

Reflect on the connection between knowing God and living out your faith. Consider the following questions:

- How do you anticipate the attributes of God we studied in Quarter 1 influencing the way you live your life?

- What is one area of your daily life where you would like to see your understanding of God make a tangible difference?

- As you look ahead to the theme of "Living Out Our Faith," what are your hopes for practical growth and application?

Devotional: Moving Forward in Our Faith Journey

Our faith is not meant to be stagnant; it is a dynamic journey of growth and application. The insights we've gained about God's character provide the "why" behind how we live. Now, as we transition into Quarter 2, we will begin to explore the "how": how we can practically embody our faith in our relationships, our decisions, and our daily routines.

This transition is an opportunity to connect the theological truths we've studied with the practical realities of our lives. May the knowledge of God's deep love compel us to love others more fully. May the experience of His grace empower us to extend grace. May the assurance of His faithfulness give us courage in uncertain times.

As we move forward, let us do so with open hearts and a willingness to allow our understanding of God to transform the way we live.

Prayer Prompt:

Spend time in prayer asking God to help you connect the knowledge you've gained about Him with the practical living out of your faith. Pray for wisdom and guidance as you begin to explore the theme of "Living Out Our Faith" in the next quarter.

Personal Reflection & Growth Journal

Significant Moments / Insights from This Week's Study

What happened? What was the insight?

_____

_____

_____

_____

_____

Emotional/Spiritual Responses:

_____

_____

_____

_____

_____

Spiritual Insights/Lessons Learned:

- First thoughts:

_____

_____

_____

_____

- New perspectives gained:

_____

_____

_____

_____

- My Response/Action:

_____

_____

_____

_____

What helped me connect with God/grow this ?week?

_____

_____

_____

_____

What hindered my connection/?growth?

_____

_____

_____

_____

Week 15: Living Out Our Faith

Having spent the initial weeks deepening our understanding of God's character, we now turn our focus to how this knowledge practically shapes our lives. Our beliefs are not meant to be confined to our minds or hearts; they are intended to permeate every aspect of our existence, influencing our actions, our relationships, and our responses to the world around us.

Think about the connection between what you believe to be true and how you live each day. Does your outward life consistently reflect the truths you hold dear? This quarter will be an invitation to more intentionally align our actions with our faith.

Scripture Prompt:

Spend time meditating on **James 2:17**:

> *"So also faith by itself, if it does not have works, is dead."*
> (ESV)

What does this verse emphasize about the relationship between faith and action? What does it mean for faith to be "dead" if it doesn't have works? How does this challenge our understanding of what it means to truly believe?

Guided Reflection:

Reflect on the theme of "Living Out Our Faith." Consider the following questions:

- What does "living out your faith" look like in your current season of life?

- What is one area where you feel a gap between what you believe and how you act?

- As we begin this quarter, what is one practical step you hope to take in living out your faith more intentionally?

Devotional: Setting Our Hearts on Practical Application

The truths we've learned about God - His love, His justice, His mercy - are not just abstract concepts; they are the very principles that should guide our interactions and decisions. This quarter, we will delve into practical ways to embody these attributes in our daily lives. We will explore themes such as love in action, forgiveness, patience, humility, and integrity.

Our aim is not to create a list of rules but to cultivate a heart that naturally reflects God's character in all we do. As we engage with Scripture and reflection prompts focused on practical application, may we grow in our ability to live out our faith authentically and impactfully.

Let us approach this quarter with a willingness to examine our lives and to allow God's Word to shape not just what we know, but how we live.

Prayer Prompt:

Spend time in prayer asking God to guide you as you explore the practical aspects of living out your faith. Pray for a heart that is eager to apply His truths to your daily life and for the strength to act in ways that honor Him.

Personal Reflection & Growth Journal

Significant Moments / Insights from This Week's Study

What happened? What was the insight?

_____

_____

_____

_____

Emotional/Spiritual Responses:

_____

_____

_____

_____

Spiritual Insights/Lessons Learned:

- First thoughts:

_____

_____

_____

- New perspectives gained:

_____

_____

_____

- My Response/Action:

_____

_____

_____

What helped me connect with God/grow this ?week?

_____
_____
_____
_____
_____

What hindered my connection/?growth?

_____
_____
_____
_____
_____

II. Quarter 2: Living Out Our Faith (Weeks 16-28) -
Theme: Practical Application in Daily Life

Week 16: Love and Kindness in Action

Having set our hearts on living out our faith, we begin by exploring the foundational principles of love and kindness. These are not merely feelings but active choices that demonstrate the heart of God to those around us. Scripture consistently emphasizes the importance of loving God and loving our neighbor as ourselves (Matthew 22:37-39). Kindness is love put into action, extending grace and care in tangible ways.

Think about the times you have experienced genuine love and kindness from others. How did it impact you? Now consider how you can intentionally extend that same care to those in your sphere of influence.

Scripture Prompt:

Spend time meditating on **1 Corinthians 13:4-7**:

> *"Love is patient and kind; love does not envy or boast; it is not arrogant or rude. It does not insist on its own way; it is not irritable or resentful; it does not rejoice at wrongdoing, but rejoices with the truth. Love bears all things, believes all things, hopes all things, endures all things."* (ESV)

Reflect on each characteristic of love described in this passage. Which of these qualities comes most naturally to you? Which do you find most challenging to embody consistently? How can you intentionally grow in demonstrating these aspects of love through your actions?

Now, also read **Galatians 5:22**:

> *"But the fruit of the Spirit is love, joy, peace, patience, kindness, goodness, faithfulness, gentleness, self-control; against such things there is no law."* (ESV)

Notice that kindness is listed as a fruit of the Spirit. What does this imply about the source of true kindness? How can you cultivate a life that is more yielded to the Holy Spirit, allowing this fruit to grow and be expressed through you?

Guided Reflection:

Write down your thoughts on the questions above and your insights from 1 Corinthians 13:4-7 and Galatians 5:22. Consider specific individuals in your life, such as family, friends, colleagues, and neighbors, and brainstorm practical ways you can show them love and kindness this week.

Devotional: Showing God's Heart Through Our Actions

Our words can express love, but our actions often speak even louder. When we intentionally choose to be patient, kind, and generous, we reflect the very nature of God to those around us. These acts of love and kindness can open doors for deeper connection and can be powerful testimonies to the transformative power of the Gospel.

This week let's be mindful of opportunities to demonstrate love and kindness in tangible ways. This might involve offering a helping hand, listening attentively, speaking encouraging words, performing a small act of service, or simply extending patience and understanding in a challenging situation.

Remember that even small acts of love and kindness, done with a sincere heart, can have a significant impact. As we intentionally choose to love and be kind, we not only bless others but also deepen our own connection with the God who is the ultimate source of love.

Prayer Prompt:

Spend time in prayer asking God to fill you with His love and to give you eyes to see opportunities to show kindness to others. Pray for a willing heart and the strength to act in ways that reflect His love in your daily interactions.

Personal Reflection & Growth Journal

Significant Moments / Insights from This Week's Study

What happened? What was the insight?

_____

_____

_____

_____

_____

Emotional/Spiritual Responses:

_____

_____

_____

_____

Spiritual Insights/Lessons Learned:

- First thoughts:

_____

_____

_____

_____

- New perspectives gained:

_____

_____

_____

_____

- My Response/Action:

_____

_____

_____

_____

What helped me connect with God/grow this ?week?

_____

_____

_____

_____

What hindered my connection/?growth?

_____

_____

_____

_____

Week 17: Forgiveness and Reconciliation

Relationships are a beautiful and essential part of life, yet they are also often the places where hurt and offense can occur. Holding onto bitterness and unforgiveness can weigh us down and hinder our connection with God and others. Forgiveness, though sometimes difficult, is a powerful act of obedience and a pathway to healing and reconciliation.

Think about any relationships in your life where there has been hurt or brokenness. Reflect on the impact of holding onto unforgiveness and the potential for freedom that forgiveness can bring.

Scripture Prompt:

Spend time meditating on **Matthew 6:14-15**:

> *"For if you forgive others their trespasses, your heavenly Father will also forgive you, but if you do not forgive others their trespasses, neither will your Father forgive your trespasses."* (ESV)

What is the direct connection Jesus makes between our forgiveness of others and God's forgiveness of us? How does this emphasize the importance of extending forgiveness? What might be the implications of holding onto unforgiveness in our relationship with God?

Now, also read **Colossians 3:13**:

> *"bearing with one another and, if one has a complaint against another, forgiving each other; as the Lord has forgiven you, so you also must forgive."* (ESV)

What does it mean to "bear with one another"? What is the motivation for forgiving others according to this verse? How does reflecting on God's forgiveness of us empower us to forgive others?

Guided Reflection:

Write down your thoughts on the questions above and your insights from Matthew 6:14-15 and Colossians 3:13. Consider any specific individuals you may need to forgive or situations where reconciliation is needed. What steps might you need to take towards forgiveness and healing?

Devotional: The Healing Power of Letting Go

Forgiveness is not about condoning wrong behavior or forgetting the hurt that was caused. Instead, it is a conscious decision to release the bitterness, resentment, and the desire for revenge that can consume us. It is an act of obedience to God and a gift we give ourselves, freeing us from the emotional bondage of the past.

Reconciliation, where possible and healthy, is the beautiful outcome of forgiveness – the restoration of broken relationships. It requires humility, vulnerability, and a willingness from all parties involved. While reconciliation may not always be possible, forgiveness is always a choice we can make.

This week let's prayerfully consider any areas in our lives where forgiveness is needed. Ask God for the courage and grace to release those who have hurt us, trusting that He is the ultimate source of justice and healing. Where appropriate, seek opportunities for reconciliation, approaching those relationships with humility and a spirit of love.

Prayer Prompt:

Spend time in prayer asking God to reveal any areas of unforgiveness in your heart. Pray for the strength and willingness to forgive those who have hurt you, just as Christ has forgiven you. If there are opportunities for reconciliation, pray for wisdom and guidance in approaching those situations.

Personal Reflection & Growth Journal

Significant Moments / Insights from This Week's Study

What happened? What was the insight?

_____

_____

_____

_____

_____

Emotional/Spiritual Responses:

_____

_____

_____

_____

Spiritual Insights/Lessons Learned:

- First thoughts:

_____

_____

_____

_____

- New perspectives gained:

_____

_____

_____

_____

- My Response/Action:

_____

_____

_____

_____

What helped me connect with God/grow this ?week?

_____

_____

_____

_____

What hindered my connection/?growth?

_____

_____

_____

_____

_____

_____

_____

_____

Week 18: Patience and Perseverance

Life is rarely a sprint; more often, it's a marathon filled with delays, obstacles, and moments that test our resolve. In these times, patience and perseverance are vital aspects of living out our faith. Patience allows us to wait with hope and a calm spirit, while perseverance empowers us to keep moving forward despite difficulties.

Think about situations in your life that require waiting or where you've faced significant challenges. Reflect on your natural response to these circumstances and the role that patience and perseverance have played.

Scripture Prompt:

Spend time meditating on **Romans 5:3-5**:

> *"Not only that, but we rejoice in our sufferings, knowing that suffering produces endurance, and endurance produces character, and character produces hope, and hope does not put us to shame, because God's love has been poured into our hearts through the Holy Spirit who has been given to us."* (ESV)

Notice the progression described in this passage. How does suffering, though difficult, ultimately lead to hope through endurance and character? What role does God's love, poured into our hearts, play in sustaining our perseverance?

Now, also read **Hebrews 12:1**:

> *"Therefore, since we are surrounded by so great a cloud of witnesses, let us also lay aside every weight, and sin which clings so closely, and let us run with endurance the race that is set before us,"* (ESV)

What imagery is used here to describe the Christian life? What does it mean to "lay aside every weight and sin"? What is the attitude with which we are called to run this "race"?

Guided Reflection:

Write down your thoughts on the questions above and your insights from Romans 5:3-5 and Hebrews 12:1. Consider specific areas where you are currently being called to exercise patience or where you need strength to persevere through challenges.

Devotional: Staying the Course with Hope

Patience is not passive resignation; it is an active waiting with expectation and trust in God's timing. It involves choosing a spirit of peace and contentment even when circumstances are not unfolding as we desire. Perseverance, on the other hand, is the steadfast determination to continue following God and pursuing His purposes, even when the path is difficult or unclear.

This week let's intentionally cultivate both patience and perseverance in our lives. When faced with delays or frustrations, let us pray for a calm and trusting heart. When confronted with obstacles, let us draw strength from God and remember the ultimate hope we have in Him.

Remember that growth often happens during seasons of waiting and through the challenges we overcome. By embracing patience and persevering in faith, we develop spiritual resilience and a deeper reliance on God's strength and timing.

Prayer Prompt:

Spend time in prayer asking God to cultivate patience within you, especially in areas where you tend to become frustrated or discouraged. Pray for the strength and determination to persevere through any challenges you are currently facing, keeping your eyes fixed on Him and the hope He provides.

Personal Reflection & Growth Journal

Significant Moments / Insights from This Week's Study

What happened? What was the insight?

_____

_____

_____

_____

_____

Emotional/Spiritual Responses:

_____

_____

_____

_____

_____

Spiritual Insights/Lessons Learned:

• First thoughts:

_____

_____

_____

_____

- New perspectives gained:

_____

_____

_____

_____

- My Response/Action:

_____

_____

_____

_____

What helped me connect with God/grow this ?week?

_____

_____

_____

_____

What hindered my connection/?growth?

_____

_____

_____

_____

Week 19: Humility and Service

Humility and service are two sides of the same coin in the Kingdom of God. Humility is recognizing our dependence on God and valuing others above ourselves, while service is the practical outworking of that humility, putting the needs of others before our own. Jesus Himself exemplified both perfectly, coming not to be served but to serve (Mark 10:45).

Think about individuals you admire for their humility and their servant hearts. Reflect on the impact of their attitude and actions. How can you cultivate these qualities more intentionally in your own life?

Scripture Prompt:

Spend time meditating on **Philippians 2:3-4**:

"Do nothing from selfish ambition or conceit, but in humility count others more significant than yourselves. Let each of you look not only to his own interests, but also to the interests of others." (ESV)

What does it mean to "count others more significant than yourselves"? How does this contrast with selfish ambition and conceit? What practical steps can you take to look not only to your own interests but also to the interests of others?

Now, also read **Mark 10:45**:

"For even the Son of Man came not to be served but to serve, and to give his life as a ransom for many." (ESV)

How does Jesus' own example shape our understanding of true leadership and greatness? What does it mean to "serve" in the context of our daily lives and relationships? How can we reflect Jesus' servant heart?

Guided Reflection:

Meditate on the questions above and your insights from Philippians 2:3-4 and Mark 10:45. Consider specific relationships or contexts where you can intentionally practice humility and service this week.

Devotional: Following the Example of Christ

True greatness in God's eyes is often found in humility and a willingness to serve. When we lay aside our pride and self-seeking desires, we create space for God to work through us and for us to genuinely connect with and uplift others. Service, done with a humble heart, is an act of love that reflects the character of Christ.

This week let's be intentional about seeking opportunities to serve those around us, whether in small, unseen ways or in more visible acts of kindness. This might involve offering help without expecting anything in return, listening attentively to someone in need, or using your gifts and talents to benefit others.

By embracing humility and cultivating a servant heart, we not only follow the example of Jesus but also experience the joy and fulfillment that comes from putting others first. This way of living transforms our relationships and allows God's love to flow through us more freely.

Prayer Prompt:

Spend time in prayer asking God to cultivate humility within you and to give you a heart that is eager to serve others. Pray for opportunities to put the needs of others before your own and for a spirit of genuine love and selflessness in your interactions.

Personal Reflection & Growth Journal

Significant Moments / Insights from This Week's Study

What happened? What was the insight?

_____

_____

_____

_____

_____

Emotional/Spiritual Responses:

_____

_____

_____

_____

Spiritual Insights/Lessons Learned:

- First thoughts:

_____

_____

_____

- New perspectives gained:

_____

_____

_____

- My Response/Action:

_____

_____

_____

_____

What helped me connect with God/grow this ?week?

_____

_____

_____

_____

What hindered my connection/?growth?

_____

_____

_____

_____

Week 20: Integrity and Honesty

Integrity and honesty are the cornerstones of a life that honors God and builds trust with others. Integrity means living in alignment with our values and beliefs, even when no one is watching. Honesty is speaking the truth, even when it's difficult or uncomfortable. These qualities reflect God's own character and are essential for authentic Christian living.

Think about individuals you know who are characterized by their integrity and honesty. Reflect on the sense of trust and respect they inspire. How can you cultivate these qualities more deeply in your own life?

Scripture Prompt:

Spend time meditating on **Proverbs 12:22**:

"Lying lips are an abomination to the Lord, but those who act faithfully are his delight." (ESV)

What strong language is used here to describe lying? What contrast is drawn with those who act faithfully? How does this verse highlight God's perspective on honesty and integrity?

Now, also read **Ephesians 4:25**:

"Therefore, having put away falsehood, let each one of you speak the truth with his neighbor, for we are members one of another." (ESV)

What clear command is given in this verse? What is the reasoning provided for speaking the truth? How does our interconnectedness as members of the body of Christ emphasize the importance of honesty?

Guided Reflection:

Write down your reflections on the questions above and your insights from Proverbs 12:22 and Ephesians 4:25. Consider specific areas of your life where you are challenged to be fully honest and to live with unwavering integrity.

Devotional: Living a Life of Truthfulness

Our words and actions have a significant impact on those around us and on our witness for Christ. When we live with integrity and speak truthfully, we build a foundation of trust in our relationships and demonstrate the trustworthiness of God. Conversely, dishonesty erodes trust and can damage our testimony.

This week let's be particularly mindful of our words and actions, striving for complete honesty in all our interactions. This includes not only avoiding outright lies but also being truthful in our motives, our promises, and our representations of ourselves. Living with integrity also means being consistent in our values, allowing our beliefs to shape our behavior in every area of life, both publicly and privately.

By committing to integrity and honesty, we honor God, strengthen our relationships, and live with a clear conscience. This way of living is a powerful reflection of the One who is truth itself (John 14:6).

Prayer Prompt:

Spend time in prayer asking God to reveal any areas in your life where you may be compromising on honesty or integrity. Pray for the courage to speak the truth, even when it's difficult, and for the strength to live in alignment with your beliefs in all circumstances.

Personal Reflection & Growth Journal

Significant Moments / Insights from This Week's Study

What happened? What was the insight?

_____

_____

_____

_____

Emotional/Spiritual Responses:

_____

_____

_____

_____

Spiritual Insights/Lessons Learned:

- First thoughts:

_____

_____

_____

- New perspectives gained:

_____

_____

_____

- My Response/Action:

_____

_____

_____

_____

What helped me connect with God/grow this ?week?

_____

_____

_____

_____

What hindered my connection/?growth?

_____

_____

_____

_____

Week 21: Generosity and Giving

Generosity and giving are more than just financial acts; they reflect a heart that understands the abundance God has provided and a willingness to share those blessings with others. Scripture encourages us to give freely, cheerfully, and with a spirit of love (2 Corinthians 9:7), recognizing that all we have ultimately comes from God.

Think about times you have experienced the joy of giving or receiving a generous gift. Reflect on the impact of generosity, both on the giver and the receiver. How can you cultivate a more generous spirit in your own life?

Scripture Prompt:

Spend time meditating on **2 Corinthians 9:6-7**:

"The point is this: whoever sows sparingly will also reap sparingly, and whoever sows bountifully will also reap bountifully. Each one must give as he has decided in his heart, not reluctantly or under compulsion, for God loves a cheerful giver." (ESV)

What principle of sowing and reaping is highlighted in this passage? What attitude should accompany our giving? What does it mean that "God loves a cheerful giver"?

Now, also read **Luke 6:38**:

"give, and it will be given to you. Good measure, pressed down, shaken together, running over, will be put into your lap. For with the measure you use it will be measured back to you."" (ESV)

What promise is given to those who give? What kind of measure is described? How does this verse encourage a generous approach to sharing our resources?

Guided Reflection:

Write down your thoughts on the questions above and your insights from 2 Corinthians 9:6-7 and Luke 6:38. Consider the various ways you can be generous – with your time, talents, and resources – and identify practical ways to give this week.

Devotional: The Joy of Sharing God's Blessings

Generosity is not about what we give but about the heart with which we give. When we recognize that all we possess is a gift from God, we are freed to share it with open hands and joyful hearts. Giving is an act of worship and an expression of our gratitude for God's provision.

This week let's be intentional about looking for opportunities to be generous. This might involve contributing financially to causes you believe in, offering your time to help someone in need, sharing your skills or talents, or simply being generous with your kindness and encouragement.

Remember that generosity extends beyond material possessions. We can also be generous with our forgiveness, our patience, our time, and our love. As we cultivate a generous spirit, we not only bless others but also experience the deep joy that comes from reflecting God's own giving nature.

Prayer Prompt:

Spend time in prayer asking God to cultivate a generous heart within you. Pray for wisdom to discern how you can best use your resources – time, talents, and finances – to bless others and honor Him. Ask for a cheerful spirit in your giving.

Personal Reflection & Growth Journal

Significant Moments / Insights from This Week's Study

What happened? What was the insight?

_____

_____

_____

_____

_____

Emotional/Spiritual Responses:

_____

_____

_____

_____

_____

Spiritual Insights/Lessons Learned:

- First thoughts:

_____

_____

_____

_____

- New perspectives gained:

_____

_____

_____

_____

• My Response/Action:

_____

_____

_____

_____

What helped me connect with God/grow this ?week?

_____

_____

_____

_____

_____

What hindered my connection/?growth?

_____

_____

_____

_____

Week 22: Prayer and Communication with God

Prayer is the lifeline of our relationship with God. It is our direct line of communication, a sacred space where we can speak to our Heavenly Father, share our hearts, seek His guidance, and express our gratitude. It's not about reciting perfect words but about authentic connection with the One who loves us unconditionally.

Think about your current prayer life. What does it look like? What are the joys and challenges you experience in communicating with God?

How can you cultivate a deeper and more consistent practice of prayer?

Scripture Prompt:

Spend time meditating on **Philippians 4:6-7**:

> *"Do not be anxious about anything, but in everything by prayer and supplication with thanksgiving let your requests be made known to God. And the peace of God, which surpasses all understanding, will guard your hearts and your minds in Christ Jesus."* (ESV)

What are we encouraged to do instead of being anxious? What elements should be part of our prayer life according to this passage? What is the promised result of bringing our requests to God with thanksgiving?

Now, also read **1 Thessalonians 5:17**:

> *"pray without ceasing."* (ESV)

What does it mean to "pray without ceasing"? Is this a call to be constantly vocal? How can we cultivate a lifestyle of continuous communication with God throughout our day?

Guided Reflection:

Write down your reflections on the questions above and your insights from Philippians 4:6-7 and 1 Thessalonians 5:17. Consider practical ways you can deepen your prayer life this week, perhaps by setting aside specific times, trying new forms of prayer, or being more mindful of God's presence throughout your day.

Devotional: Cultivating a Conversation with the Divine

Prayer is a multifaceted conversation with God. It includes adoration for who He is, confession of our sins, thanksgiving for His blessings, and supplication for our needs and the needs of others. It's a time to listen for His still, small voice and to align our hearts with His will.

This week let's be intentional about cultivating a richer prayer life. This might involve setting aside dedicated time each day for focused prayer, keeping a prayer journal, praying Scripture back to God, or simply having ongoing conversations with Him as you go about your day.

Remember that God longs to hear from you. He is not distant or uninterested but is intimately involved in your life. By making prayer a consistent priority, we open ourselves to His guidance, comfort, and peace that surpasses all understanding.

Prayer Prompt:

Spend time in prayer asking God to deepen your desire for communication with Him. Pray for discipline and consistency in your prayer life. Ask for guidance in how to pray more effectively and for a greater awareness of His presence as you pray.

Personal Reflection & Growth Journal

Significant Moments / Insights from This Week's Study

What happened? What was the insight?

_____

_____

_____

_____

_____

Emotional/Spiritual Responses:

_____

_____

_____

_____

Spiritual Insights/Lessons Learned:

- First thoughts:

_____

_____

_____

- New perspectives gained:

_____

_____

_____

_____

- My Response/Action:

_____

_____

_____

_____

What helped me connect with God/grow this ?week?

_____

_____

_____

_____

_____

What hindered my connection/?growth?

_____

_____

_____

_____

_____

Week 23: Wisdom in Decision Making

Life is a series of choices, both big and small. As we seek to live out our faith, it's crucial to approach these decisions with wisdom – the ability to discern what is right and good, and to make choices that align with God's will and His principles. God promises to give wisdom to those who ask (James 1:5), and Scripture provides guidance for navigating the complexities of life.

Think about significant decisions you've faced. How did you seek wisdom? What were the outcomes? Reflect on the importance of making choices that honor God and lead to good outcomes.

Scripture Prompt:

Spend time meditating on **James 1:5**:

> *"If any of you lacks wisdom, let him ask God, who gives generously to all without reproach, and it will be given him."* (ESV)

What encouragement and promise does this verse offer regarding wisdom? What is the condition for receiving wisdom from God? What does it mean that God gives "generously" and "without reproach"?

Now, also read **Proverbs 4:7**:

> *"The beginning of wisdom is this: Get wisdom, and whatever you get, get insight."* (ESV)

What does this proverb identify as the "beginning of wisdom"? What does it emphasize about the importance of actively seeking not just knowledge but also understanding (insight)?

Guided Reflection:

Write down your answers for the questions above and your insights from James 1:5 and Proverbs 4:7. Consider any current decisions you are facing and how you can intentionally seek God's wisdom in making them.

Devotional: Seeking God's Guidance in Our Choices

Making wise decisions involves more than just logic and reasoning; it requires seeking God's perspective through prayer, studying His Word, and listening to the counsel of godly individuals. It's about aligning our desires with His will and choosing paths that lead to righteousness and blessing.

This week let's be intentional about seeking God's wisdom in the decisions we face, both large and small. Before making a choice, take time to pray and ask for His guidance. Consider what Scripture says about the matter or related principles. Seek advice from trusted Christian mentors or friends.

Remember that God's wisdom often transcends our immediate understanding. Trusting in Him means being willing to follow His leading, even when it doesn't always make sense to us in the moment. By consistently seeking His wisdom, we can navigate life's complexities with greater clarity and confidence.

Prayer Prompt:

Spend time in prayer asking God for wisdom and discernment in the decisions you are currently facing. Pray for clarity of mind, a heart that is open to His will, and the courage to follow His leading, even when it's challenging.

Personal Reflection & Growth Journal

Significant Moments / Insights from This Week's Study

What happened? What was the insight?

_____

_____

_____

_____

_____

Emotional/Spiritual Responses:

_____

_____

_____

_____

_____

Spiritual Insights/Lessons Learned:

- First thoughts:

_____

_____

_____

- New perspectives gained:

_____

_____

_____

- My Response/Action:

_____

_____

_____

_____

What helped me connect with God/grow this ?week?

_____

_____

_____

_____

What hindered my connection/?growth?

_____

_____

_____

_____

Week 24: Managing Our Thoughts and Emotions

Our thoughts and emotions have a powerful influence on our actions and our overall well-being. As we seek to live out our faith, it's essential to learn how to manage them in a way that honors God and reflects His peace. This doesn't mean suppressing our feelings, but rather understanding them, processing them healthily, and aligning them with biblical truth.

Think about the times your thoughts or emotions have led you astray or caused you distress. Reflect on the importance of bringing them under the Lordship of Christ and cultivating a mind and heart that are at peace.

Scripture Prompt:

Spend time meditating on **Philippians 4:8**:

> *"Finally, brothers, whatever is true, whatever is honorable, whatever is just, whatever is pure, whatever is lovely, whatever is commendable, if there is any excellence, if there is anything worthy of praise, think about these things."* (ESV)

What specific categories of thoughts are we encouraged to focus on? How does intentionally directing our thoughts in this way impact our emotions and our overall perspective?

Now, also read **Proverbs 4:23**:

> *"Keep your heart with all vigilance, for from it flows the springs of life."* (ESV)

In this context, "heart" often refers to the inner person, including thoughts and emotions. What strong instruction is given regarding the keeping of our hearts? Why is this so important according to this verse?

Guided Reflection:

Think about the answers you would give for the questions above and your insights from Philippians 4:8 and Proverbs 4:23. Consider specific patterns of negative thinking or challenging emotions you experience. What practical steps can you take this week to intentionally direct your thoughts and guard your heart?

Devotional: Cultivating a Mind of Peace and Truth

Managing our thoughts and emotions is an ongoing process that requires intentionality and reliance on the Holy Spirit. It involves recognizing when our thoughts are not aligned with truth, challenging negative or unhelpful thought patterns, and choosing to focus on what is good, pure, and praiseworthy.

This week let's be more aware of the thoughts that occupy our minds and the emotions that stir within us. When negative thoughts arise, consciously replace them with biblical truths and affirmations. When strong emotions surface, take time to process them in a healthy way, perhaps through prayer, journaling, or talking with a trusted friend.

Remember that we have the mind of Christ (1 Corinthians 2:16) and the power of the Holy Spirit to help us in this area. By intentionally choosing to dwell on what is true and good, and by entrusting our emotions to God, we can cultivate a greater sense of inner peace and live in a way that honors Him.

Prayer Prompt:

Spend time in prayer asking God to give you greater awareness of your thought patterns and emotional responses. Pray for His help in challenging negative thoughts and replacing them with His truth. Ask for His peace to guard your heart and mind in Christ Jesus.

Personal Reflection & Growth Journal

Significant Moments / Insights from This Week's Study

What happened? What was the insight?

_____

_____

_____

_____

_____

Emotional/Spiritual Responses:

_____

_____

_____

_____

Spiritual Insights/Lessons Learned:

- First thoughts:

_____

_____

_____

- New perspectives gained:

_____

_____

_____

- My Response/Action:

_____

_____

_____

_____

What helped me connect with God/grow this ?week?

_____

_____

_____

_____

_____

What hindered my connection/?growth?

_____

_____

_____

_____

_____

Week 25: Our Words and Their Impact

Our words hold immense power: the power to build up or tear down, to encourage or discourage, to speak truth or to deceive. As followers of Christ, our speech should reflect His love, grace, and truth. We are called to be mindful of the impact our words have on those around us and to use them in ways that honor God and bless others.

Think about times when someone's words deeply impacted you, for good or for ill. Reflect on the responsibility we have to use our words thoughtfully and intentionally.

Scripture Prompt:

Spend time meditating on **James 3:5-10**:

"So also the tongue is a small member, yet it boasts of great things. How great a forest is set ablaze by a small fire! And the tongue is a fire, a world of unrighteousness set among our members, staining the whole body, setting on fire the entire course of life, and set on fire by hell. For every kind of beast and bird, of reptile and sea creature, can be tamed and has been tamed by mankind, but no human being can tame the tongue. It is a restless evil, full of deadly poison. With it we bless our Lord and Father, and with it we curse human beings who are made in the likeness of God. From the same mouth come blessing and cursing. My brothers, these things ought not to be so." (ESV)

What powerful and sobering imagery does James use to describe the tongue? What does this passage reveal about the potential for both good and harm in our words? What is the inconsistency James highlights in how we often use our tongues?

Now, also read **Proverbs 15:1**:

"A soft answer turns away wrath, but a harsh word stirs up anger." (ESV)

What practical wisdom does this proverb offer regarding our communication, particularly in conflict? How can choosing our words carefully influence the outcome of a conversation?

Guided Reflection:

Write down your answers for the questions above and your insights from James 3:5-10 and Proverbs 15:1. Consider your own patterns of speech. Are there areas where you need to be more mindful of the impact of your words? What practical steps can you take this week to speak with more grace and truth?

Devotional: Speaking Life and Truth

Our words are a reflection of what is in our hearts (Matthew 12:34). As we grow in our relationship with God, our speech should increasingly reflect His character. This means speaking with kindness, encouragement, and truth. It involves choosing words that build up rather than tear down, that offer hope rather than despair, and that honor God in all circumstances.

This week let's be intentional about the words we speak. Before we speak, let us consider their potential impact. Are they true? Are they kind? Are they necessary? Let us strive to be those who speak life and truth into the lives of others, using our words as instruments of God's love and grace.

Remember that even seemingly small words can have a lasting effect. Let us choose to use them wisely, reflecting the heart of the One who is the Word of life.

Prayer Prompt:

Spend time in prayer asking God to help you be more mindful of the words you speak. Pray for a filter on your tongue, that your words would be seasoned with grace and truth. Ask for wisdom in knowing when to speak and when to remain silent, and for the power to use your words to bless and encourage others.

Personal Reflection & Growth Journal

Significant Moments / Insights from This Week's Study

What happened? What was the insight?

_____

_____

_____

_____

_____

Emotional/Spiritual Responses:

_____

_____

_____

_____

_____

Spiritual Insights/Lessons Learned:

- First thoughts:

_____

_____

_____

_____

- New perspectives gained:

_____

_____

_____

_____

- My Response/Action:

_____

_____

_____

_____

What helped me connect with God/grow this ?week?

_____

_____

_____

_____

What hindered my connection/?growth?

_____

_____

_____

_____

Week 26: Rest and Sabbath

In our busy, productivity-driven culture, the concept of rest can often feel like a luxury rather than a necessity. However, God Himself modeled rest after creation (Genesis 2:2-3) and commanded a Sabbath for His people. Observing a rhythm of rest is not just about physical rejuvenation; it's an act of trust in God's provision and a recognition that our worth is not solely tied to our accomplishments.

Think about your own patterns of rest. Do you intentionally set aside time to cease from your regular work and activities? What are the challenges you face in prioritizing rest? Reflect on the potential spiritual and physical benefits of embracing a Sabbath rhythm.

Scripture Prompt:

Spend time meditating on **Mark 2:27**:

> *"And he said to them, "The Sabbath was made for man, not man for the Sabbath.""* (ESV)

What does Jesus mean by this statement? How does it shift the focus of the Sabbath? What is the intended purpose of rest according to Jesus?

Now, also read **Hebrews 4:9-10**:

> *"So then, there remains a Sabbath rest for the people of God, for whoever has entered God's rest has also rested from his works as God did from his."* (ESV)

What kind of "Sabbath rest" remains for God's people? How does entering God's rest relate to ceasing from our own works? What does this imply about our ultimate rest in Christ?

Guided Reflection:

Consider your answers for the questions above and your insights from Mark 2:27 and Hebrews 4:9-10. Consider how you can intentionally incorporate more rest and perhaps a Sabbath practice into your week. What might need to shift in your schedule or mindset to prioritize this?

Devotional: Finding Renewal in Ceasing

Rest, especially a dedicated Sabbath, is an opportunity to step back from the demands of our work and responsibilities and to intentionally focus on God and the things that truly nourish our souls. It's a time for physical refreshment, spiritual renewal, and relational connection.

This week, consider how you can intentionally create space for rest. This might involve setting aside a specific day or portion of a day to cease from your usual work, to spend time in prayer and reflection, to enjoy peaceful activities, and to connect with loved ones.

Remember that rest is not laziness; it is an act of obedience and a recognition of our human limits and God's unlimited provision. By embracing a rhythm of rest, we honor God, care for ourselves, and return to our responsibilities with renewed energy and perspective.

Prayer Prompt:

Spend time in prayer asking God to reveal any areas where you are neglecting rest. Pray for wisdom to prioritize rest in a way that honors Him and nourishes your soul. Ask for guidance in establishing healthy rhythms of work and rest in your life.

Personal Reflection & Growth Journal

Significant Moments / Insights from This Week's Study

What happened? What was the insight?

_____

_____

_____

_____

_____

Emotional/Spiritual Responses:

_____

_____

_____

_____

_____

Spiritual Insights/Lessons Learned:

- First thoughts:

_____

_____

_____

_____

- New perspectives gained:

_____

_____

_____

_____

- My Response/Action:

_____

_____

_____

_____

What helped me connect with God/grow this ?week?

_____

_____

_____

_____

_____

What hindered my connection/?growth?

_____

_____

_____

_____

_____

Week 27: Sharing Our Faith

As those who have experienced the love and truth of God, we are called to share this good news with others. Sharing our faith isn't about forceful proselytizing but about authentically communicating the hope we have in Christ through our words and actions. It's about allowing our lives to be a testimony to God's grace and being ready to articulate the reasons for our belief when opportunities arise.

Think about the moment you came to faith or a time when your faith became particularly meaningful to you. Reflect on the desire to share that with others and the ways you have (or haven't yet) done so.

Scripture Prompt:

Spend time meditating on **Matthew 28:19-20**:

> *"Go therefore and make disciples of all nations, baptizing them in the name of the Father and of the Son and of the Holy Spirit, teaching them to observe all that I have commanded you. And behold, I am with you always, to the end of the age."* (ESV)

What is the Great Commission that Jesus gives His followers? What are the key components of making disciples? What promise does Jesus give alongside this command?

Now, also read **1 Peter 3:15**:

> *"but in your hearts honor Christ the Lord as holy, always being prepared to make a defense to anyone who asks you for a reason for the hope that is in you; yet do it with gentleness and respect."* (ESV)

What does it mean to "honor Christ the Lord as holy" in our hearts? What posture should we have in sharing our faith? What attitude should accompany our defense of the hope we have?

Guided Reflection:

Write down your reflections on the questions above and your insights from Matthew 28:19-20 and 1 Peter 3:15. Consider the people in your life who may not yet know Christ. What are some ways you can authentically share your faith with them through your words and actions this week?

Devotional: Letting Our Light Shine

Sharing our faith is not about having all the answers or being a perfect theologian. It's about allowing the light of Christ within us to shine outwardly. Our transformed lives, our acts of love and kindness, and our willingness to speak about the hope we have can all be powerful witnesses to God's grace.

This week let's be prayerfully open to opportunities to share our faith. This might involve sharing a personal testimony, explaining why you follow Christ, inviting someone to church, or simply living in such a way that others see the difference Christ makes in your life.

Remember that God doesn't call us to convert people but to faithfully share the truth in love. Trust the Holy Spirit to work in hearts, and be ready to speak with gentleness and respect when the opportunity arises.

Prayer Prompt:

Spend time in prayer asking God for boldness and wisdom in sharing your faith. Pray for opportunities to speak about His love and truth, and for the right words to say. Ask for a heart that desires others to know the joy and peace you have found in Christ.

Personal Reflection & Growth Journal

Significant Moments / Insights from This Week's Study

What happened? What was the insight?

_____

_____

_____

_____

_____

Emotional/Spiritual Responses:

_____

_____

_____

_____

_____

Spiritual Insights/Lessons Learned:

- First thoughts:

_____

_____

_____

- New perspectives gained:

_____

_____

_____

- My Response/Action:

_____

_____

_____

_____

What helped me connect with God/grow this ?week?

_____

_____

_____

_____

What hindered my connection/?growth?

_____

_____

_____

_____

Week 28: Review and Reflection on Living Out Faith

Over the past twelve weeks, we've focused on the practical ways our faith in God should shape our daily lives. We've explored themes such as love, forgiveness, patience, humility, honesty, generosity, prayer, wisdom, managing our thoughts, our words, rest, and sharing our faith. This week is an opportunity to look back, reflect on what we've learned, and consider how we are growing in embodying these principles.

Think about the various areas of your life we've touched upon. In which of these areas have you felt challenged? Where have you seen growth? What resonates most with you as essential for living out your faith authentically?

Scripture Prompt:

Spend time meditating on **Galatians 2:20**:

> *"I have been crucified with Christ. It is no longer I who live, but Christ who lives in me. And the life I now live in the flesh I live by faith in the Son of God, who loved me and gave himself for me."* (ESV)

How does this verse encapsulate the essence of living out our faith? What does it mean for Christ to live in us? How does this truth connect with the practical themes we've explored this quarter?

Guided Reflection:

Think about the themes of "Living Out Our Faith" explored in Weeks 16 through 27. Consider the following questions:

- Which of the practical applications of faith we studied this quarter felt most relevant to your current season of life? Why?

- In what area of living out your faith do you sense the most significant growth over the past few weeks? What contributed to that growth?

- What is one area where you feel God is still calling you to more intentional action in living out your faith? What might be a first step in that direction?

- How has reflecting on these practical aspects deepened your understanding of what it means to follow Christ in your everyday life?

Devotional: Continuing to Embody Our Beliefs

Living out our faith is not a destination but a continuous journey of growth and refinement. The principles we've explored this quarter are not meant to be mastered in a few weeks but rather to become ongoing practices that shape our character and our interactions with the world.

As we move towards the next quarter, let us carry with us the lessons learned about loving, forgiving, persevering, serving, being honest, giving generously, praying consistently, seeking wisdom, managing our inner lives, using our words wisely, prioritizing rest, and sharing our hope.

May we continue to be intentional in allowing our beliefs to translate into tangible actions, reflecting the love and light of Christ in all we do.

Prayer Prompt:

Spend time in prayer asking God to help you integrate the principles of living out your faith into your daily life. Pray for continued growth in these areas and for a heart that is eager to embody His love and truth in all your actions and interactions.

Personal Reflection & Growth Journal

Significant Moments / Insights from This Week's Study

What happened? What was the insight?

_____

_____

_____

_____

_____

Emotional/Spiritual Responses:

_____

_____

_____

_____

_____

Spiritual Insights/Lessons Learned:

- First thoughts:

_____

_____

_____

- New perspectives gained:

_____

_____

_____

_____

• My Response/Action:

_____

_____

_____

_____

What helped me connect with God/grow this ?week?

_____

_____

_____

_____

_____

What hindered my connection/?growth?

_____

_____

_____

_____

_____

III. Quarter 3: Connecting with Others (Weeks 29-41) - Theme: Our Relationships and Community

Week 29: Our Relationships and Community

Having spent the last quarter focusing on how our individual faith impacts our actions and choices, we now turn our attention to the relational aspect of our faith journey. Quarter 3 will explore the theme of "Connecting with Others." As believers, we are part of a larger body, the Church, and our relationships with one another are vital for support, encouragement, and reflecting the love of Christ to the world.

Think about the significance of community in your faith. How have others influenced your walk with God? How do you see your role in the lives of fellow believers and those around you?

Scripture Prompt:

Spend time meditating on **1 John 4:7**:

> *"Beloved, let us love one another, for love is from God, and whoever loves has been born of God and knows God."*
> (ESV)

What is the clear command given in this verse regarding our relationships with one another? What is the connection made between love and our relationship with God? How does this emphasize the importance of love within the Christian community?

Guided Reflection:

Think about the theme of "Connecting with Others." Consider the following questions:

- What does "Christian community" mean to you? What are some of the benefits and challenges of being part of a faith community?

- How do you currently connect with other believers for encouragement and support? Are there ways you would like to deepen these connections?

- As you look ahead to exploring our relationships and community in Quarter 3, what are your hopes for growth in this area?

Devotional: The Importance of Godly Connections

God designed us for relationships, both with Him and with one another. Within the community of believers, we find encouragement, accountability, support in times of need, and the opportunity to serve and be served. Our interactions with fellow Christians and even those outside our immediate faith community are meant to reflect the love and unity that characterize the body of Christ.

As we begin this quarter, let us open our hearts to the importance of building and nurturing godly connections. We will explore themes such as the value of community, healthy friendships, navigating family relationships, extending grace, resolving conflict, and the impact of our witness on those around us.

May this quarter be a time of growth in our ability to love and connect with others in ways that honor God and strengthen the fabric of His Kingdom.

Prayer Prompt:

Spend time in prayer asking God to highlight the importance of your relationships within the body of Christ and beyond. Pray for wisdom and guidance in building healthy and meaningful connections with others. Ask for a heart that is open to loving and serving those around you.

Personal Reflection & Growth Journal

Significant Moments / Insights from This Week's Study

What happened? What was the insight?

_____

_____

_____

_____

Emotional/Spiritual Responses:

_____

_____

_____

_____

Spiritual Insights/Lessons Learned:

- First thoughts:

_____

_____

_____

- New perspectives gained:

_____

_____

_____

- My Response/Action:

_____

_____

_____

_____

What helped me connect with God/grow this ?week?

_____

_____

_____

_____

_____

What hindered my connection/?growth?

_____

_____

_____

_____

Week 30: The Importance of Christian Community

After introducing the theme of connecting with others, we begin by focusing on the Christian community itself. The Bible often describes believers as a body with many parts (1 Corinthians 12:12-27), a family (Ephesians 2:19), and living stones building a spiritual house (1 Peter 2:5). We are not meant to navigate our faith journey in isolation but in supportive fellowship with other believers.

Think about your current experiences with Christian community. What are the benefits you've personally found in being connected with other believers? What challenges or obstacles have you encountered in seeking or maintaining community?

Scripture Prompt:

Spend time meditating on **Hebrews 10:24-25**:

> *"And let us consider how to stir up one another to love and good works, not neglecting to meet together, as is the habit of some, but encouraging one another, and all the more as you see the Day drawing near."* (ESV)

What is the purpose of meeting together as believers according to this passage? What does it mean to "stir up one another to love and good works"? How does the approaching "Day" (referring to Christ's return) emphasize the urgency of Christian fellowship?

Now, also read **Acts 2:42-47** (focus on verses 42 and 46-47):

> *"And they devoted themselves to the apostles' teaching and the fellowship, to the breaking of bread and the prayers... And day by day, attending the temple together and breaking bread in their homes, they received their food with glad and generous hearts, praising God and having favor with all the people. And the Lord added to their number day by day those who were being saved."* (ESV)

What were the early believers devoted to? What characteristics describe their fellowship and shared life? What was the outcome of their strong community and devotion?

Guided Reflection:

Write down your reflections on the questions above and your insights from Hebrews 10:24-25 and Acts 2:42-47. Consider your involvement in Christian community. What is one practical step you can take this week to more fully engage with or contribute to a healthy Christian community?

Devotional: Finding Strength and Support in the Body

Christian community is a vital gift from God. It's where we are challenged, encouraged, comforted, and sharpened. Within this fellowship, we can share our burdens, celebrate our victories, grow through accountability, and learn from the diverse perspectives and gifts of others. It is where we find a sense of belonging and truly experience being part of God's family.

This week let's intentionally consider the importance of Christian community in our lives. If you are already actively involved, give thanks for those relationships and look for ways to deepen them. If you are not yet connected, prayerfully consider seeking out a church or small group where you can find genuine fellowship and support.

Remember, we are not designed to live out our faith alone. Just as individual threads woven together create a strong tapestry, believers united in Christ form a powerful testimony to God's love and work in the world.

Prayer Prompt:

Spend time in prayer thanking God for the gift of Christian community. Pray for your local church or Christian fellowship, asking God to strengthen it and to use it for His glory. If you are seeking community, pray for His guidance in finding the right place of belonging and growth.

Personal Reflection & Growth Journal

Significant Moments / Insights from This Week's Study

What happened? What was the insight?

_____

_____

_____

_____

_____

Emotional/Spiritual Responses:

_____

_____

_____

_____

_____

Spiritual Insights/Lessons Learned:

- First thoughts:

_____

_____

_____

_____

- New perspectives gained:

_____

_____

_____

_____

- My Response/Action:

_____

_____

_____

_____

What helped me connect with God/grow this ?week?

_____

_____

_____

_____

_____

What hindered my connection/?growth?

_____

_____

_____

_____

Week 31: Building Healthy Friendships

Healthy friendships add richness and depth to our lives, providing support, encouragement, and shared experiences along our faith journey. They offer a space for vulnerability, accountability, and mutual growth.

Think about the friends who have had a positive impact on your life. What qualities do they possess that make those friendships meaningful? How do healthy friendships contribute to your spiritual growth and overall well-being?

Scripture Prompt:

Spend time meditating on **Proverbs 17:17**:

"A friend loves at all times, and a brother is born for adversity." (ESV)

What does it mean for a friend to love "at all times"? How does this contrast with fair-weather acquaintances? How does the second part of this proverb broaden our understanding of the depth and purpose of true friendship?

Now, also read **1 Thessalonians 5:11**:

"Therefore encourage one another and build one another up, just as you are doing." (ESV)

What is the primary action we are called to in our interactions with one another? How do encouragement and building up contribute to healthy friendships within the community of believers?

Guided Reflection:

Write down your reflections on the questions above and your insights from Proverbs 17:17 and 1 Thessalonians 5:11. Consider the friendships in your life. Are they characterized by consistent love and mutual encouragement? What steps can you take to nurture existing friendships or build new, healthy connections within your community?

Devotional: Cultivating Meaningful Connections

Healthy friendships are a precious gift. They provide a safe space for vulnerability, honest feedback, shared laughter, and mutual support through life's challenges and triumphs. Building these kinds of connections requires intentionality, time, and a willingness to be both a giver and a receiver in the relationship.

This week, consider reaching out to a friend you appreciate. Perhaps schedule time to connect over a meal, take a walk together, or simply send a message of encouragement. Be mindful of being a good listener and offering support in practical ways.

Remember that friendships, like any valuable thing, need tending to flourish. Invest time and effort in nurturing the relationships God has placed in your life, and be open to the possibility of new, meaningful connections with those around you.

Prayer Prompt:

Spend time in prayer thanking God for the gift of friendship. Pray for your current friends, asking for strength and blessing in their lives. Ask for wisdom in nurturing these relationships and for guidance in building new, healthy friendships with those around you.

Personal Reflection & Growth Journal

Significant Moments / Insights from This Week's Study

What happened? What was the insight?

_____

_____

_____

_____

_____

Emotional/Spiritual Responses:

_____

_____

_____

_____

_____

Spiritual Insights/Lessons Learned:

- First thoughts:

_____

_____

_____

- New perspectives gained:

_____

_____

_____

_____

- My Response/Action:

_____

_____

_____

_____

What helped me connect with God/grow this ?week?

_____

_____

_____

_____

_____

What hindered my connection/?growth?

_____

_____

_____

_____

_____

Week 32: Navigating Family Relationships

Family relationships, whether by blood or by choice, are some of the most significant and often the most complex connections in our lives. They can be sources of immense joy and support, but also of deep-seated challenges and unique dynamics. Living out our faith in the context of family requires grace, understanding, patience, and a willingness to extend unconditional love.

Think about the various family relationships in your life. What are the unique blessings they offer? What are some of the particular challenges you encounter in these relationships, and how do you typically navigate them?

Scripture Prompt:

Spend time meditating on **Ephesians 4:2-3**:

> *"with all humility and gentleness, with patience, bearing with one another in love, eager to maintain the unity of the Spirit in the bond of peace."* (ESV)

What specific virtues are we called to practice in our relationships? How do "bearing with one another in love" and "eager to maintain the unity of the Spirit" apply particularly to the, often intense, dynamics of family?

Now, also read **Colossians 3:12-14**:

> *"Put on then, as God's chosen ones, holy and beloved, compassionate hearts, kindness, humility, meekness, and patience, bearing with one another and, if one has a complaint against another, forgiving each other; as the Lord has forgiven you, so you also must forgive. And above all these put on love, which binds everything together in perfect harmony."* (ESV)

Many of these attributes overlap with ones we've already discussed. Why are they so crucial for healthy family interactions? How does "love, which binds everything together in perfect harmony," serve as the ultimate goal for our family relationships?

Guided Reflection:

Think about the questions above and your insights from Ephesians 4:2-3 and Colossians 3:12-14. Identify a couple family relationships where you want to apply these biblical principles more intentionally this week. What specific actions or changes in attitude can you focus on?

Devotional: Grace at Home

Our homes and families are often the truest testing grounds of our faith. It's easy to extend kindness and patience to strangers, but it can be much harder to do so with those who know us best, and whose imperfections, like our own, are most visible. Yet, it is precisely in these intimate relationships that our faith can shine most brightly and bring about the most profound impact.

This week let's commit to bringing "grace at home." This means actively choosing to listen, to respond with gentleness rather than reactivity, to offer forgiveness freely, and to seek understanding. It means recognizing that every member of your family is a person created in God's image, worthy of respect and love, regardless of past hurts or current challenges.

Remember that God is the author of family, and He desires for these relationships to flourish. By intentionally seeking to embody His love, patience, and forgiveness within our family dynamics, we contribute to an atmosphere of peace and mutual growth.

Prayer Prompt:

Spend time in prayer for your family relationships. Ask God for wisdom, patience, and love to navigate them well. Pray for healing in any strained relationships and for strength to extend grace and forgiveness as Christ has extended it to you.

Personal Reflection & Growth Journal

Significant Moments / Insights from This Week's Study

What happened? What was the insight?

_____

_____

_____

_____

_____

Emotional/Spiritual Responses:

_____

_____

_____

_____

Spiritual Insights/Lessons Learned:
  • First thoughts:

_____

_____

_____

- New perspectives gained:

_____

_____

_____

_____

- My Response/Action:

_____

_____

_____

_____

What helped me connect with God/grow this ?week?

_____

_____

_____

_____

What hindered my connection/?growth?

_____

_____

_____

_____

_____

_____

_____

_____

Week 33: Extending Grace to Others

We've explored God's abundant grace towards us, and now we turn to the vital practice of extending that same grace to the people around us. Grace is unmerited favor, a gift given freely, not because it's earned but because of a generous heart. In our interactions, extending grace means offering understanding, patience, and forgiveness, even when it's not deserved, reflecting God's own heart towards us.

Think about a time someone showed you unexpected grace when you made a mistake or fell short. How did that act of grace make you feel? Consider the opportunities you have in your daily life to offer grace to those you encounter.

Scripture Prompt:

Spend time meditating on **Ephesians 4:32**:

> *"Be kind to one another, tenderhearted, forgiving one another, as God in Christ forgave you."* (ESV)

What specific actions are we called to practice in our relationships? What is the ultimate motivation or standard for our forgiveness of others? How does understanding God's forgiveness of you empower you to extend it to others?

Now, also read **Romans 15:7**:

> *"Therefore welcome one another as Christ has welcomed you, for the glory of God."* (ESV)

What does it mean to "welcome one another as Christ has welcomed you"? How does extending such welcome contribute to the glory of God? How can this verse guide your interactions with new acquaintances or those who might be different from you in our diverse city?

Guided Reflection:

Think about the questions above and your insights from Ephesians 4:32 and Romans 15:7. Identify one specific person or situation this week where you can intentionally choose to extend grace, perhaps by overlooking a minor irritation, offering understanding instead of judgment, or showing unexpected kindness.

Devotional: The Ripple Effect of Unmerited Favor

Extending grace is not always easy. Our natural inclination can be to react with judgment, frustration, or a desire for fairness. However, when we choose grace, we step into the divine, mirroring the boundless mercy God has shown us. This act transforms not only the recipient but also our own hearts, freeing us from bitterness and allowing God's peace to flow through us.

This week let's look for opportunities to be agents of grace in our interactions. This might involve being patient with a difficult colleague, offering a second chance to someone who disappointed you, giving someone the benefit of the doubt, or simply responding with calm when faced with rudeness. It's about remembering that everyone you meet is a complex individual, often facing unseen struggles, and is worthy of compassion.

Remember, the grace we extend is a powerful testimony to the grace we have received from God. Let it be a beautiful overflow of His unmerited favor in your life, creating a ripple effect of kindness and understanding in your community and beyond.

Prayer Prompt:

Spend time in prayer asking God to fill you with a spirit of grace and compassion. Pray for opportunities to extend unmerited favor to those around you, and for a heart that is quick to forgive and slow to judge, just as He is with you.

Personal Reflection & Growth Journal

Significant Moments / Insights from This Week's Study

What happened? What was the insight?

_____

_____

_____

_____

Emotional/Spiritual Responses:

_____

_____

_____

_____

Spiritual Insights/Lessons Learned:

- First thoughts:

_____

_____

_____

- New perspectives gained:

_____
_____
_____
_____

- My Response/Action:

_____
_____
_____
_____

What helped me connect with God/grow this ?week?

_____
_____
_____
_____

What hindered my connection/?growth?

_____
_____
_____
_____

Week 34: Resolving Conflict Biblically

Even in the most loving communities, misunderstandings and disagreements are inevitable. Conflict, when handled poorly, can lead to deep hurt and broken relationships. However, when approached biblically, conflict can become an opportunity for growth, deeper understanding, and stronger bonds. God's Word provides clear guidance on how to navigate disagreements in a way that honors Him and fosters reconciliation.

Think about a recent conflict or disagreement you experienced. How did you react? What was the outcome? Reflect on how often personal or community peace is impacted by how conflict is handled, from the smallest daily interactions to larger community issues.

Scripture Prompt:

Spend time meditating on **Matthew 18:15**:

> *"If your brother sins against you, go and tell him his fault, between you and him alone. If he listens to you, you have gained your brother."* (ESV)

What is the first step Jesus instructs us to take when a conflict arises? Why is it emphasized that this should be done "between you and him alone"? What is the positive outcome if this step is successful?

Now, also read **Ephesians 4:26-27**:

> *"Be angry and do not sin; do not let the sun go down on your anger, and give no opportunity to the devil."* (ESV)

What important distinction is made regarding anger? What practical instruction is given about addressing anger? How does unresolved anger create an "opportunity for the devil" in our relationships?

Guided Reflection:

Write down your answers for the questions above and consider your insights from Matthew 18:15 and Ephesians 4:26-27. Think about a specific ongoing or past conflict in your life. What biblical principles from these verses can you apply to that situation? What is one step you can take toward biblical conflict resolution this week?

Devotional: Pursuing Peace and Understanding

Biblical conflict resolution is rooted in humility, a desire for reconciliation, and a commitment to truth spoken in love. It requires us to address issues directly and privately when possible, to listen empathetically, to confess our own part in the conflict, and to be quick to forgive as God has forgiven us. It is a proactive approach to maintaining peace and preserving relationships.

This week let's commit to addressing conflicts in a way that honors God. When tensions arise, pause and pray for wisdom and self-control. Seek to understand the other person's perspective before defending your own. Choose to speak truthfully, but always with kindness and respect. Remember that the goal is not to win an argument, but to restore a relationship and bring glory to God.

By engaging in biblical conflict resolution, we contribute to healthier relationships in our families, churches, workplaces, and broader communities. We become agents of peace, reflecting Christ in our interactions, even in the midst of disagreement.

Prayer Prompt:

Spend time in prayer for any specific conflicts you are currently navigating. Ask God for humility, courage, and wisdom to address these situations biblically. Pray for a spirit of reconciliation and for His peace to prevail in your relationships.

Personal Reflection & Growth Journal

Significant Moments / Insights from This Week's Study

What happened? What was the insight?

_____

_____

_____

_____

_____

Emotional/Spiritual Responses:

_____

_____

_____

_____

Spiritual Insights/Lessons Learned:

- First thoughts:

_____

_____

_____

_____

- New perspectives gained:

_____

_____

_____

_____

- My Response/Action:

_____

_____

_____

_____

What helped me connect with God/grow this ?week?

_____

_____

_____

_____

_____

What hindered my connection/?growth?

_____

_____

_____

_____

Week 35: Hospitality and Welcoming Others

True Christian connection often extends beyond our immediate circles to embrace those who are new, different, or in need of a place to belong. Hospitality is more than just offering a meal; it's a spirit of warmth, openness, and genuine welcome that reflects God's own heart towards us. It's about creating space in our lives and homes for others, fostering a sense of belonging and community.

Think about a time you felt truly welcomed and included. What made that experience special? Conversely, recall a time you felt excluded. How did that impact you? Reflect on how you currently practice hospitality in your daily life.

Scripture Prompt:

Spend time meditating on **Romans 12:13**:

> *"Contribute to the needs of the saints and seek to show hospitality."* (ESV)

What two actions are linked together in this verse? What does it imply about the nature of contributing to needs and showing hospitality? How can this verse encourage a proactive approach to welcoming others?

Now, also read **Hebrews 13:2**:

> *"Do not neglect to show hospitality to strangers, for thereby some have entertained angels unawares."* (ESV)

Why is it important not to "neglect to show hospitality to strangers"? What surprising possibility is mentioned regarding welcoming those we don't know? How does this verse broaden our understanding of whom we are called to welcome?

Guided Reflection:

Write down your reflections on the questions above and your insights from Romans 12:13 and Hebrews 13:2. Consider the people around you, perhaps new colleagues, neighbors, or someone sitting alone at a gathering. What is one practical step you can take this week to extend hospitality and make someone feel truly welcome?

Devotional: Opening Our Hearts and Homes

Hospitality is a powerful way to express God's love. It breaks down barriers, builds bridges, and fosters authentic relationships. It can be as simple as offering a warm smile, striking up a conversation with someone you don't know well, or inviting a new acquaintance for coffee. It might also involve opening your home for a meal, a conversation, or a time of fellowship.

This week let's cultivate a spirit of genuine welcome. Look for opportunities to go out of your way to make others feel seen, valued, and included. This might mean initiating a conversation, inviting someone into your space, or simply paying attention to those who seem overlooked. Remember that showing hospitality is not about impressing others; it's about serving them and demonstrating the inclusive love of

Christ.

By intentionally practicing hospitality, we not only bless those we welcome but also enrich our own lives and deepen our understanding of God's heart for all people. It's an active way to live out our faith in community.

Prayer Prompt:

Spend time in prayer asking God for a hospitable heart. Pray for eyes to see those around you who might need a word of welcome or a gesture of inclusion. Ask for courage and wisdom to extend hospitality in ways that honor Him and bless others.

Personal Reflection & Growth Journal

Significant Moments / Insights from This Week's Study

What happened? What was the insight?

_____

_____

_____

_____

_____

Emotional/Spiritual Responses:

_____

_____

_____

_____

Spiritual Insights/Lessons Learned:

- First thoughts:

_____

_____

_____

_____

- New perspectives gained:

_____

_____

_____

_____

- My Response/Action:

_____

_____

_____

_____

What helped me connect with God/grow this ?week?

_____

_____

_____

_____

What hindered my connection/?growth?

_____

_____

_____

_____

Week 36: Encouraging and Building Up Others

In a world that can often be critical or demanding, the power of encouragement is immense. As followers of Christ, we are called to be instruments of God's grace, actively seeking to uplift, affirm, and strengthen those around us. Encouragement is a vital expression of love and a powerful way to build up the body of believers and positively impact our wider communities.

Think about a time when someone's words of encouragement made a significant difference in your life or helped you through a challenging period. What was the impact of their affirmation? Now, consider how you can intentionally be a source of encouragement for others.

Scripture Prompt:

Spend time meditating on **Ephesians 4:29**:

> *"Let no corrupting talk come out of your mouths, but only such as is good for building up, as fits the occasion, that it may give grace to those who hear."* (ESV)

What kind of talk are we commanded to avoid? What kind of speech are we to cultivate instead? What is the purpose of our words ("building up") and their effect ("give grace to those who hear")? How can this verse guide your conversations this week?

Now, also read **1 Thessalonians 5:11**:

> *"Therefore encourage one another and build one another up, just as you are doing."* (ESV)

What is the direct command given regarding our interactions within the community? What does it mean to "build one another up"? How does this verse emphasize that encouragement is a shared responsibility among believers?

Guided Reflection:

Write down your reflections on the questions above and your insights from Ephesians 4:29 and 1 Thessalonians 5:11. Consider specific individuals in your life, such as family members, friends, colleagues, or fellow churchgoers, who might need a word of encouragement this week. What specific words or actions could you offer to build them up?

Devotional: The Gift of Affirmation

Encouragement is a divine gift that breathes life and hope into others. It acknowledges their value, affirms their efforts, and reminds them of God's presence and power in their lives. It's about seeing the potential in others, celebrating their strengths, and gently supporting them through their struggles. This isn't about flattery, but about genuine, heartfelt affirmation rooted in love and truth.

This week let's intentionally look for opportunities to speak life-giving words. Listen attentively for moments when someone expresses doubt, faces a challenge, or feels overlooked. Take a moment to offer sincere praise, express gratitude, or simply remind them of God's faithfulness.

This might involve a verbal affirmation, a thoughtful message, or a specific act of support.

Remember that a single word of encouragement can transform a person's day, strengthen their spirit, and inspire them to persevere. By making encouragement a regular practice, we become channels of God's grace, reflecting His heart that always seeks to uplift and restore.

Prayer Prompt:

Spend time in prayer asking God to give you a heart that is quick to encourage and affirm others. Pray for discernment to know when and how to speak words of life. Ask for the courage to step out and build up those around you, reflecting His love and hope.

Personal Reflection & Growth Journal

Significant Moments / Insights from This Week's Study

What happened? What was the insight?

_____

_____

_____

_____

_____

Emotional/Spiritual Responses:

_____

_____

_____

_____

_____

Spiritual Insights/Lessons Learned:

- First thoughts:

_____

_____

_____

_____

- New perspectives gained:

_____

_____

_____

_____

- My Response/Action:

_____

_____

_____

_____

What helped me connect with God/grow this ?week?

_____

_____

_____

_____

What hindered my connection/?growth?

_____

_____

_____

_____

Week 37: Being a Faithful Friend and Ally

As we continue to explore connecting with others, we delve into the active role of being a faithful friend and ally. This means more than just being present during good times; it involves loyalty, trustworthiness, and standing with others, especially when they face challenges or injustice.

Think about what it truly means to be a loyal friend. Have you had experiences where someone stood by you unconditionally? How did that impact your sense of security and belonging? Consider how you can embody this faithfulness in your own relationships.

Scripture Prompt

Spend time meditating on **Proverbs 18:24**:

> *"A man of many companions may come to ruin, but there is a friend who sticks closer than a brother."* (ESV)

What contrast is drawn here between casual acquaintances and a true friend? What does it mean for a friend to "stick closer than a brother"? How does this proverb highlight the value of deep, faithful friendships?

Now, also read **Galatians 6:2**:

> *"Bear one another's burdens, and so fulfill the law of Christ."* (ESV)

What practical action are we called to perform for one another? What does it mean to "bear one another's burdens"? How does this act of supportive friendship fulfill "the law of Christ," which is often understood as the law of love?

Guided Reflection

Write down your reflections on the questions above and your insights from Proverbs 18:24 and Galatians 6:2. Consider a specific friend or community member whom you can intentionally support or stand with this week. How might you practically "bear their burden" or demonstrate your loyalty?

Devotional: Standing Steadfast with Others

Being a faithful friend and ally means choosing commitment over convenience. It involves listening without judgment, offering practical help when needed, speaking truth in love, and defending those who are vulnerable. This kind of loyalty is a powerful reflection of God's steadfastness towards us. It's about being a safe and reliable presence for others, especially during difficult times.

This week let's look for opportunities to practice faithful friendship. This might involve reaching out to someone who is struggling, advocating for someone who is being unfairly treated, or simply being a consistent and trustworthy presence in someone's life. Think about how you can offer a tangible form of support or encouragement.

Remember that loyalty builds trust, and trust forms the bedrock of strong relationships. By choosing to be faithful friends and allies, we not only strengthen our personal connections but also contribute to a more compassionate and supportive community, mirroring the faithfulness of Christ.

Prayer Prompt

Spend time in prayer asking God for the strength and courage to be a faithful friend and ally to those around you. Pray for discernment to know when and how to bear others' burdens. Ask for a heart that is loyal and trustworthy, reflecting His own steadfast love.

Personal Reflection & Growth Journal

Significant Moments / Insights from This Week's Study

What happened? What was the insight?

_____

_____

_____

_____

_____

Emotional/Spiritual Responses:

_____

_____

_____

_____

Spiritual Insights/Lessons Learned:

- First thoughts:

_____

_____

_____

- New perspectives gained:

_____

_____

_____

• My Response/Action:

_____

_____

_____

_____

What helped me connect with God/grow this ?week?

_____

_____

_____

_____

What hindered my connection/?growth?

_____

_____

_____

_____

Week 38: Practicing Empathy and Understanding

Building strong connections with others requires more than just being present; it demands the ability to step into another person's shoes, to genuinely understand their feelings, and to see the world from their perspective. This is the essence of **empathy**. It's a compassionate response that validates others' experiences, even when we don't fully agree or comprehend.

Think about a time someone truly "got" you, making you feel heard and understood. How did that impact your relationship with them? Now, consider situations where you've struggled to understand another person's viewpoint or emotions. What made it difficult?

Scripture Prompt

Spend time meditating on **Romans 12:15**:

> *"Rejoice with those who rejoice; weep with those who weep."* (ESV)

What does this verse call us to do in relation to others' emotions? What does it mean to truly "rejoice with" or "weep with" someone, rather than just observing their feelings? How does this active participation in others' emotional experiences demonstrate empathy?

Now, also read **1 Peter 3:8**:

> *"Finally, all of you, have unity of mind, sympathy, brotherly love, a tender heart, and a humble mind."* (ESV)

Notice the cluster of qualities mentioned here, including "sympathy" (which is closely related to empathy) and a "tender heart." How do these qualities contribute to our ability to understand and connect with others? Why is a "humble mind" essential for truly understanding another's perspective?

Guided Reflection

Write down your reflections on the questions above and your insights from Romans 12:15 and 1 Peter 3:8. Consider a specific relationship or interaction where you can intentionally practice empathy this week. What questions can you ask to better understand their perspective? How can you genuinely validate their feelings, even if you don't share them?

Devotional: The Bridge of Understanding

Empathy builds a bridge between people, allowing us to connect on a deeper, more meaningful level. It moves beyond just hearing someone's words to truly grasping the emotions and experiences behind them. This doesn't mean we have to agree with every perspective, but it does mean we strive to understand and respond with compassion.

This week let's make a conscious effort to practice empathy in our daily interactions. When someone is speaking, listen not just to respond, but to understand. Ask clarifying questions. Pay attention to non-verbal cues. If someone shares a struggle, resist the urge to immediately offer solutions or advice, and instead, first offer a listening ear and a validating presence. If they share a joy, celebrate genuinely with them.

Remember, empathy is a powerful expression of love. By choosing to understand and connect with others on an emotional level, we reflect the compassionate heart of God, who fully understands our weaknesses and rejoices in our joys.

Prayer Prompt

Spend time in prayer asking God to give you a heart of empathy and a spirit of understanding. Pray for the ability to truly listen and connect with others on a deeper level. Ask for compassion for those who are struggling and genuine joy for those who are celebrating.

Personal Reflection & Growth Journal

Significant Moments / Insights from This Week's Study

What happened? What was the insight?

_____

_____

_____

_____

_____

Emotional/Spiritual Responses:

_____

_____

_____

_____

Spiritual Insights/Lessons Learned:

- First thoughts:

_____

_____

_____

_____

- New perspectives gained:

_____
_____
_____
_____

- My Response/Action:

_____
_____
_____
_____

What helped me connect with God/grow this ?week?

_____
_____
_____
_____

What hindered my connection/?growth?

_____
_____
_____
_____

Week 39: Valuing Diversity and Unity

The world, and indeed our vibrant city, is a tapestry woven with countless different threads – cultures, backgrounds, perspectives, and gifts. As believers, we are called not only to acknowledge this diversity but to truly value it as a reflection of God's creative genius. At the same time, we are commanded to strive for unity in Christ, recognizing that our common faith transcends all differences. Valuing diversity without sacrificing unity, and pursuing unity without erasing unique identities, is a profound expression of godly love.

Think about the various people you encounter in your daily life – perhaps at work, in your neighborhood, or in your spiritual community. How do you respond to those who are different from you? Reflect on the beauty of a diverse group coming together in harmony.

Scripture Prompt

Spend time meditating on **Galatians 3:28**:

> *"There is neither Jew nor Gentile, neither slave nor free, nor is there male and female, for you are all one in Christ Jesus."* (ESV)

What significant distinctions does Paul declare are no longer divisive "in Christ Jesus"? What does this verse teach about the foundation of our unity as believers? How does this spiritual reality challenge any human-made divisions we might hold?

Now, also read **Romans 15:5-7**:

> *"May the God of endurance and encouragement grant you to live in such harmony with one another, in accord with Christ Jesus, that together you may with one voice glorify the God and Father of our Lord Jesus Christ. Therefore welcome one another as Christ has welcomed you, for the glory of God."* (ESV)

What is the ultimate goal of living in "harmony with one another"? How does welcoming each other, despite differences, lead to glorifying God? What is the divine source of this harmony and endurance?

Guided Reflection

Write down your reflections on the questions above and your insights from Galatians 3:28 and Romans 15:5-7. Consider a specific group or individual whose background or perspective is different from your own. How can you actively seek to understand, value, and build bridges with them this week, reflecting the unity we have in Christ?

Devotional: The Richness of God's Design

God delights in variety, and His creation is a testament to His boundless imagination. This diversity extends to humanity, where each person is uniquely gifted and wonderfully made. When we come together as believers, our different strengths, experiences, and cultural expressions contribute to a richer, more complete picture of who God is and how He works. Unity is not uniformity; it's a harmonious blending of distinct parts, all working together for a common purpose – to glorify God.

This week let's intentionally seek to value the diversity within our spiritual community and the wider world. Engage in conversations with those who hold different perspectives. Listen to their stories. Seek to understand their traditions and backgrounds. Look for ways to celebrate the unique contributions each person brings, while always holding fast to the foundational truths that unite us in Christ.

Remember, the Kingdom of God is a place where every tongue, tribe, and nation will worship together. By practicing unity in diversity now, we participate in His glorious eternal plan.

Prayer Prompt

Spend time in prayer thanking God for the beautiful diversity among people. Pray for a heart that genuinely values and appreciates differences. Ask for wisdom to pursue unity within your spiritual community, breaking down barriers and fostering harmony that reflects Christ.

Personal Reflection & Growth Journal

Significant Moments / Insights from This Week's Study

What happened? What was the insight?

_____

_____

_____

_____

_____

Emotional/Spiritual Responses:

_____

_____

_____

_____

Spiritual Insights/Lessons Learned:

- First thoughts:

_____

_____

_____

_____

- New perspectives gained:

_____

_____

_____

_____

- My Response/Action:

_____

_____

_____

_____

What helped me connect with God/grow this ?week?

_____

_____

_____

_____

What hindered my connection/?growth?

_____

_____

_____

_____

Week 40: Being a Good Neighbour and Citizen

Our faith is not just lived within the walls of our homes or places of worship; it is profoundly expressed in how we engage with our broader community and society. Being a good neighbor and a responsible citizen means actively contributing to the well-being of our surroundings, seeking justice, promoting peace, and demonstrating love to all, regardless of their beliefs or backgrounds. This proactive engagement reflects God's heart for His creation and His desire for shalom (wholeness and peace) in all areas of life.

Think about your immediate neighborhood or the wider societal context you live in. What needs do you observe? How do you currently contribute to the flourishing of your community? Reflect on the ways your faith compels you to be involved beyond your personal circle.

Scripture Prompt

Spend time meditating on **Jeremiah 29:7**:

> *"But seek the welfare of the city where I have sent you into exile, and pray to the Lord on its behalf, for in its welfare you will find your welfare."* (ESV)

Though written in a specific historical context, what timeless principle does this verse convey about our engagement with the place God has put us? What two actions are we called to take for the welfare of our community? How does seeking the welfare of our community ultimately benefit us?

Now, also read **Romans 13:1**:

> *"Let every person be subject to the governing authorities. For there is no authority except from God, and those that exist have been instituted by God."* (ESV)

What general instruction is given regarding governing authorities? What is the divine basis for this instruction? How does this verse inform our approach to our civic responsibilities, such as obeying laws and participating thoughtfully in society?

Guided Reflection

Reflect on the questions above and your insights from Jeremiah 29:7 and Romans 13:1. Consider a specific area in your neighborhood or community where you can actively seek its welfare this week. This might be a small act of kindness, engaging in a local initiative, or simply being a more attentive and caring presence.

Devotional: Contributing to the Common Good

Our faith calls us to be salt and light in the world (Matthew 5:13-16), preserving what is good and illuminating truth. Being a good neighbor and citizen is a practical way to fulfill this calling. It means being mindful of our impact, participating responsibly in civic life, and looking for opportunities to serve beyond our immediate needs. This could involve volunteering, supporting local businesses, respecting public spaces, or simply being a considerate presence where you live and work.

This week let's intentionally consider how we can contribute to the common good. Engage with local news or community concerns. Look for ways to connect with your neighbors. Think about how your actions, even small ones, can foster a more thriving, peaceful, and just environment for everyone.

Remember that God is concerned with justice, peace, and the flourishing of all people. By actively participating as good neighbors and citizens, we become His hands and feet, working towards the redemption and transformation of our world.

Prayer Prompt

Spend time in prayer for your neighborhood and the broader community or city you live in. Pray for its welfare, its leaders, and for justice and peace to prevail. Ask God to show you specific ways you can be a good neighbor and citizen, actively contributing to the common good and reflecting His love.

Personal Reflection & Growth Journal

Significant Moments / Insights from This Week's Study

What happened? What was the insight?

_____

_____

_____

_____

_____

Emotional/Spiritual Responses:

_____

_____

_____

_____

_____

Spiritual Insights/Lessons Learned:
- First thoughts:

_____

_____

_____

_____

- New perspectives gained:

_____

_____

_____

_____

- My Response/Action:

_____

_____

_____

_____

What helped me connect with God/grow this ?week?

_____

_____

_____

_____

What hindered my connection/?growth?

_____

_____

_____

_____

Week 41: Review and Reflection on Connecting with Others

Over the past twelve weeks, we've focused on the vital theme of "Connecting with Others." We've explored the importance of Christian community, building healthy friendships, navigating complex family relationships, extending grace, resolving conflict biblically, practicing empathy, valuing diversity, and being good neighbors and citizens. This week is a dedicated time to pause, reflect, and consider how these principles have shaped our interactions and strengthened our relationships.

Think back over the various relational aspects we've discussed. In which of these areas have you felt challenged to grow? Where have you seen God work in your relationships? What new insights have you gained about reflecting Christ in your connections with others?

Scripture Prompt

Spend time meditating on **John 13:34-35**:

> *"A new commandment I give to you, that you love one another: just as I have loved you, you also are to love one another. By this all people will know that you are my disciples, if you have love for one another."* (ESV)

What is the "new commandment" Jesus gives? What is the standard for this love? What is the intended outcome or testimony of believers loving one another? How does this passage summarize the essence of what we've explored this quarter about connecting with others?

Guided Reflection

Write down your reflections on the questions above and your insights from John 13:34-35. Consider the following:

- Which specific lesson from this quarter on "Connecting with Others" has made the most significant impact on your interactions?

- In what ways have you been able to extend God's love, grace, or understanding to others more intentionally?

- What is one area of your relational life where you sense God is still calling you to greater growth or transformation? What might be the next step?

- How has focusing on these aspects of connection deepened your appreciation for the body of Christ and your role within it?

Devotional: The Ongoing Work of Relationship

Connecting with others in a way that honors God is a lifelong journey, marked by continuous learning, humility, and reliance on the Holy Spirit. The principles we've discussed this quarter are not one-time applications but habits and attitudes to be cultivated over time. Our relationships are living, breathing entities that require ongoing care, attention, and grace.

As we conclude this quarter, let us carry forward the commitment to build healthy relationships, extend genuine welcome, resolve conflict with humility, and be a faithful presence in our communities. May our interactions with family, friends, neighbors, and even strangers be a clear reflection of the love of Christ that lives within us.

May God continue to empower you to love others as He has loved you, drawing them closer to Him through the authenticity and beauty of your connections.

Prayer Prompt

Spend time in prayer thanking God for the gift of relationships and for the growth you've experienced in connecting with others this quarter. Pray for a heart that continuously seeks to love others as Christ loves. Ask for His guidance and strength to navigate all your relationships in a way that brings Him glory.

Personal Reflection & Growth Journal

Significant Moments / Insights from This Week's Study

What happened? What was the insight?

_____

_____

_____

_____

_____

Emotional/Spiritual Responses:

_____

_____

_____

_____

_____

Spiritual Insights/Lessons Learned:

- First thoughts:

_____

_____

_____

- New perspectives gained:

_____

_____

_____

_____

- My Response/Action:

_____

_____

_____

_____

What helped me connect with God/grow this ?week?

_____

_____

_____

_____

What hindered my connection/?growth?

_____

_____

_____

_____

IV. Quarter 4: Living with Purpose (Weeks 42-52) -
Theme: Discovering and Fulfilling God's Calling

Week 42: Living with Purpose

Having spent time deepening our knowledge of God and learning to live out our faith in our relationships, we now move into a profound exploration of **purpose**. This quarter, "Living with Purpose," invites us to consider God's unique calling for each of us. It's about discovering how our gifts, passions, and experiences can align with His greater plan for us and for the world around us.

Think about moments when you've felt a strong sense of meaning or direction in your life. What was happening? Reflect on the longing we all have to know why we are here and to make a meaningful difference.

Scripture Prompt

Spend time meditating on **Ephesians 2:10**:

> *"For we are his workmanship, created in Christ Jesus for good works, which God prepared beforehand, that we should walk in them."* (ESV)

What does it mean that we are God's "workmanship"? What is the purpose for which we were "created in Christ Jesus"? How does the phrase "God prepared beforehand" affect your understanding of your own life's journey? What does it imply about the intentionality of God's plan for you?

Guided Reflection

Use your journal or a notebook to record your reflections on the questions above and your insights from Ephesians 2:10. Consider your life thus far. Can you identify any "good works" that God seems to have prepared for you, even if you didn't recognize them as such at the time? How might embracing this truth influence your perspective on your future?

Devotional: Called to Live Intentionally

Every person is uniquely designed by God with specific gifts, talents, and a story to tell. Our purpose isn't something we create out of thin air; it's something we discover as we draw closer to our Creator. It's about aligning our lives with His will, using what He's given us to serve Him and others. This quarter will help us explore how our daily choices, our careers, our relationships, and our passions can all be avenues through which we fulfill God's calling.

This week, begin to approach your life with an attitude of curiosity and surrender. Ask God to reveal His purposes for you, starting with the very next steps. Pay attention to what breaks your heart, what ignites your passion, and what unique abilities you possess. These can often be clues to where God is calling you to walk in the "good works" He has prepared.

Remember, living with purpose brings profound joy and fulfillment. It's not about perfection, but about faithfully seeking and responding to God's lead, knowing that every act done in His name has eternal significance.

Prayer Prompt

Spend time in prayer asking God to reveal His purpose for your life. Pray for clarity, direction, and a heart that is eager to walk in the good works He has prepared for you. Ask for a renewed sense of meaning and intention in your daily tasks.

Personal Reflection & Growth Journal

Significant Moments / Insights from This Week's Study

What happened? What was the insight?

_____

_____

_____

_____

_____

Emotional/Spiritual Responses:

_____

_____

_____

_____

_____

Spiritual Insights/Lessons Learned:

- First thoughts:

_____

_____

_____

_____

- New perspectives gained:

_____

_____

_____

_____

- My Response/Action:

_____

_____

_____

_____

What helped me connect with God/grow this ?week?

_____

_____

_____

_____

_____

What hindered my connection/?growth?

_____

_____

_____

_____

_____

Week 43: Discovering Your Gifts and Talents

Every individual is uniquely wired by God, endowed with a distinct set of gifts, talents, and abilities. These are not random; they are intentional tools given to us to fulfill His purposes and contribute to the flourishing of the world around us. Discovering and understanding your unique gifting is a crucial step in aligning your life with God's calling and living with a profound sense of purpose. Whether your strengths lie in creativity, leadership, compassion, practical skills, or deep insight, each plays a vital role in the tapestry of human endeavor.

Think about what comes naturally to you, what you enjoy doing, or what others consistently affirm in you. Reflect on areas where you feel a sense of competence or where you instinctively know how to help.

Scripture Prompt

Spend time meditating on **1 Corinthians 12:4-7**:

> *"Now there are varieties of gifts, but the same Spirit; and there are varieties of service, but the same Lord; and there are varieties of activities, but it is the same God who empowers them all in everyone. To each is given the manifestation of the Spirit for the common good."* (ESV)

What does this passage emphasize about the *source* of our gifts and talents? What is the ultimate *purpose* for which these gifts are given? How does this verse highlight the diversity within unity when it comes to giftedness?

Now, also read **Romans 12:6-8**:

> *"Having gifts that differ according to the grace given to us, let us use them: if prophecy, in proportion to our faith; if service, in our serving; the one who teaches, in his teaching; the one who exhorts, in his exhortation; the one who contributes, in generosity; the one who leads, with zeal; the one who does acts of mercy, with cheerfulness."* (ESV)

This passage lists various gifts. What is the overarching instruction given for each of them? What does it imply about the importance of actively *using* the gifts we've been given, rather than neglecting them?

Guided Reflection

Write down your reflections on the questions above and your insights from 1 Corinthians 12:4-7 and Romans 12:6-8. List some of the gifts, talents, or strengths you believe God has given you. How have you used them recently? How might you use them more intentionally for the "common good" this week?

Devotional: Unleashing Your God-Given Potential

Discovering your gifts isn't just about identifying what you're good at; it's about recognizing how God has uniquely equipped you to bring His light into the world. Sometimes our gifts are obvious, honed through education or practice. Other times, they are subtle inclinations or burdens we feel for specific needs. The journey of purpose begins by acknowledging that you are wonderfully made and uniquely endowed.

This week, commit to a deeper exploration of your gifts. Pay attention to moments when you feel most alive and useful. Ask trusted friends or mentors what strengths they see in you. Reflect on past experiences where you made a difference. Most importantly, ask God to reveal His specific design for you and how He wants you to use it.

Remember, every gift, no matter how seemingly small, is significant in God's eyes. By embracing and utilizing our God-given abilities, we participate in His ongoing work and experience the profound joy of living out His intended purpose for our lives.

Prayer Prompt

Spend time in prayer thanking God for the unique gifts and talents He has given you. Pray for clarity and discernment to fully understand how you are wired. Ask for courage and opportunities to faithfully use your gifts for His glory and for the benefit of others.

Personal Reflection & Growth Journal

Significant Moments / Insights from This Week's Study

What happened? What was the insight?

_____

_____

_____

_____

_____

Emotional/Spiritual Responses:

_____

_____

_____

_____

_____

Spiritual Insights/Lessons Learned:

- First thoughts:

_____

_____

_____

_____

- New perspectives gained:

_____

_____

_____

_____

- My Response/Action:

_____

_____

_____

_____

What helped me connect with God/grow this ?week?

_____

_____

_____

_____

What hindered my connection/?growth?

_____

_____

_____

_____

Week 44: Serving God and Others

Having recognized our unique gifts and talents, the next step in living with purpose is to actively deploy them in service to God and others. Our purpose is rarely found in isolation; it flourishes in the context of contributing to something larger than ourselves. Whether it's through grand gestures or daily acts of kindness, serving is the tangible expression of our faith and a powerful way to reflect God's love to the world, impacting lives right here in our vibrant communities.

Think about a time when you served someone else, and it brought you unexpected joy or fulfillment. What was that experience like? Consider the various needs you see around you, both big and small, and how your gifts might address them.

Scripture Prompt

Spend time meditating on **Mark 10:45**:

> *"For even the Son of Man came not to be served but to serve, and to give his life as a ransom for many."* (ESV)

What does Jesus' own example teach us about the essence of true greatness and purpose? How does His sacrificial service inform our understanding of what it means to serve others?

Now, also read **Matthew 25:40**:

> *"And the King will answer them, 'Truly, I say to you, as you did it to one of the least of these my brothers, you did it to me.'"* (ESV)

What profound connection does Jesus make between serving "the least of these" and serving Him directly? How does this elevate the significance of every act of service, no matter how small?

Guided Reflection

Write down your answers for the questions above and your insights from Mark 10:45 and Matthew 25:40. Identify specific areas or needs in your life, church, or community where you could offer your gifts in service this week. Consider both formal and informal opportunities.

Devotional: The Joy of a Serving Heart

Serving God and others is not a burdensome duty, but a privilege and a pathway to profound joy. When we use our time, energy, and gifts to meet the needs of those around us, we step into the very heart of God, who is Himself a servant. It's in giving that we truly receive, and in pouring ourselves out for others that we find our lives filled with meaning.

This week let's intentionally look for opportunities to serve. This might involve volunteering your time in a local initiative, offering practical help to a friend or neighbor, sharing your skills at your church, or simply being attentive to moments where a kind word or a listening ear is needed. Don't underestimate the power of seemingly small acts; they can have immense impact.

Remember that every act of service, done with a sincere heart for God, has eternal value. By cultivating a serving heart, we not only live out our purpose but also become tangible expressions of Christ's love in a world desperately in need.

Prayer Prompt

Spend time in prayer asking God to give you a servant's heart and to open your eyes to the needs around you. Pray for wisdom to know how best to use your gifts in service to Him and to others. Ask for the joy that comes from generous giving of yourself.

Personal Reflection & Growth Journal

Significant Moments / Insights from This Week's Study

What happened? What was the insight?

_____

_____

_____

_____

_____

Emotional/Spiritual Responses:

_____

_____

_____

_____

_____

Spiritual Insights/Lessons Learned:

- First thoughts:

_____

_____

_____

_____

- New perspectives gained:

_____

_____

_____

_____

- My Response/Action:

_____

_____

_____

_____

What helped me connect with God/grow this ?week?

_____

_____

_____

_____

What hindered my connection/?growth?

_____

_____

_____

_____

Week 45: Cultivating a Kingdom Mindset

As we deepen our understanding of purpose and service, it's essential to cultivate a "Kingdom mindset." This means seeing beyond our immediate circumstances and personal aspirations to God's overarching plan for humanity and the world. It's about understanding that our individual purpose is intrinsically linked to His larger Kingdom purpose - bringing justice, love, and redemption to every sphere of life. This perspective shifts our focus from mere self-fulfillment to actively participating in God's ongoing work, impacting our community and beyond.

Think about how your daily decisions are influenced by your understanding of God's Kingdom. Do you consider the broader implications of your actions? Reflect on the difference it makes when you view your life not just through a personal lens, but through the lens of God's redemptive plan.

Scripture Prompt

Spend time meditating on **Matthew 6:33**:

> *"But seek first the kingdom of God and his righteousness, and all these things will be added to you."* (ESV)

What is the primary pursuit Jesus instructs us to have? What does it mean to "seek first the kingdom of God and his righteousness"? What promise accompanies this pursuit? How does this verse guide our priorities in living a purposeful life?

Now, also read **Romans 14:17**:

> *"For the kingdom of God is not a matter of eating and drinking but of righteousness and peace and joy in the Holy Spirit."* (ESV)

What does this verse clarify the Kingdom of God *is not* about? What are the true characteristics of the Kingdom of God? How does understanding these characteristics shape our pursuit of purpose and influence our interactions in the world?

Guided Reflection

Write down your reflections on the questions above and your insights from Matthew 6:33 and Romans 14:17. Consider a specific area of your life: your work, your finances, your hobbies, or your relationships. How can you more intentionally align this area with a Kingdom mindset this week, prioritizing righteousness, peace, and joy in the Holy Spirit?

Devotional: Living for a Greater Story

A Kingdom mindset transforms how we view our lives. It liberates us from the endless pursuit of personal gain and invites us into a grander narrative – God's story of redemption. When we truly grasp that we are co-laborers with Him, every task, every conversation, and every decision can become an act of worship and a contribution to His eternal purposes. This perspective helps us navigate challenges with resilience and celebrate successes with gratitude, knowing that all things are ultimately for His glory.

This week, challenge yourself to think with a Kingdom mindset. When you're making a decision, ask, "How does this align with God's righteousness? Will it bring peace? Will it foster joy in the Holy Spirit?" Look for opportunities to act justly, love mercy, and walk humbly, knowing these are expressions of the Kingdom here on Earth. Consider the specific challenges or injustices in your community or in the wider world and prayerfully consider how God might want you to respond within His Kingdom framework.

Remember, living with a Kingdom mindset allows us to experience profound fulfillment, knowing that our lives are part of something eternal and infinitely meaningful. It's an invitation to join God in His ongoing work of bringing His reign to bear on every corner of creation.

Prayer Prompt

Spend time in prayer asking God to give you a deeper understanding and a consistent application of a Kingdom mindset. Pray for your eyes to see His purposes in the world and for your heart to be aligned with His righteousness, peace, and joy. Ask for boldness to live for His Kingdom above all else.

Personal Reflection & Growth Journal

Significant Moments / Insights from This Week's Study

What happened? What was the insight?

_____

_____

_____

_____

_____

Emotional/Spiritual Responses:

_____

_____

_____

_____

Spiritual Insights/Lessons Learned:
- First thoughts:

_____

_____

_____

_____

- New perspectives gained:

_____

_____

_____

_____

- My Response/Action:

_____

_____

_____

_____

What helped me connect with God/grow this ?week?

_____

_____

_____

_____

What hindered my connection/?growth?

_____

_____

_____

_____

Week 46: Overcoming Obstacles with Faith

Living a purposeful life, aligned with God's calling, doesn't mean the absence of challenges. In fact, pursuing God's will often brings its own set of obstacles, setbacks, and moments of doubt. However, our faith provides the foundation and strength to navigate these difficulties, seeing them not as roadblocks to our purpose, but as opportunities for growth, deeper reliance on God, and clearer revelation of His power.

Think about a significant obstacle you've faced in the past. How did you respond? Did your faith play a role in overcoming it? Reflect on any current challenges that feel daunting, and consider how a faith-filled perspective might change your approach.

Scripture Prompt

Spend time meditating on **Philippians 4:13**:

> *"I can do all things through him who strengthens me."* (ESV)

What powerful affirmation does Paul make in this verse? What is the source of this strength? How does this verse empower us to face difficulties when pursuing God's calling?

Now, also read **Romans 8:28**:

> *"And we know that for those who love God all things work together for good, for those who are called according to his purpose."* (ESV)

What profound assurance is given to those who love God and are called according to His purpose? Does "all things" imply the absence of difficulty, or something deeper? How does this verse encourage perseverance and trust in God's sovereignty even amidst setbacks?

Guided Reflection

Reflect on the questions above and your insights from Philippians 4:13 and Romans 8:28. Identify a specific obstacle (personal, professional, or spiritual) you are currently facing or anticipate. How can you apply the truths from these scriptures to that situation this week? What specific action can you take, trusting in God's strength and purpose?

Devotional: Faith as Our Anchor in the Storm

Obstacles are an inherent part of the human journey, but for those living with purpose in Christ, they are not insurmountable. Our faith acts as an anchor, holding us steady when the winds of adversity blow. It reminds us that God is bigger than any problem, that His strength is made perfect in our weakness, and that He is always working for our good and His glory, even when circumstances seem chaotic. Overcoming with faith isn't about wishing problems away, but facing them with courage, resilience, and a deep trust in God's unfailing presence and power.

This week, when you encounter a challenge, pause and remember God's promises. Instead of succumbing to fear or discouragement, actively seek His perspective. Ask Him for the strength, wisdom, and creativity to navigate the situation. Lean into your community for support and prayer. See if this obstacle might be a divinely orchestrated opportunity for you to grow, learn, or witness to God's faithfulness.

Remember, every obstacle overcome by faith strengthens your character and deepens your testimony. You are not alone in this journey; the God who called you is faithful to equip and sustain you through every trial, ultimately working all things for good towards His purposes.

Prayer Prompt

Spend time in prayer for any specific obstacles or challenges you are currently facing. Ask God for unwavering faith to overcome them. Pray for His strength to be evident in your weakness, for His wisdom to guide your steps, and for the peace that comes from trusting in His ultimate plan.

Personal Reflection & Growth Journal

Significant Moments / Insights from This Week's Study

What happened? What was the insight?

_____

_____

_____

_____

_____

Emotional/Spiritual Responses:

_____

_____

_____

_____

Spiritual Insights/Lessons Learned:

- First thoughts:

_____

_____

_____

_____

- New perspectives gained:

_____

_____

_____

_____

- My Response/Action:

_____

_____

_____

_____

What helped me connect with God/grow this ?week?

_____

_____

_____

_____

What hindered my connection/?growth?

_____

_____

_____

_____

Week 47: Stewarding Your Resources for God's Kingdom

Living with purpose extends to how we manage every aspect of our lives, including finances and possessions. Stewarding our resources for God's Kingdom means recognizing that everything we have is ultimately a gift from Him, entrusted to us to be used for His glory and the advancement of His purposes. It's about prioritizing generosity, living responsibly, and making wise choices with what God has given us, acknowledging that we are managers, not owners. This applies whether we are considering our personal budget or contributing to initiatives that uplift our communities.

Think about your current approach to managing your resources. Do you view them as solely yours, or as gifts entrusted to you by God? Reflect on how your financial and material choices align with your faith and your sense of purpose.

Scripture Prompt

Spend time meditating on **2 Corinthians 9:7-8**:

> *"Each one must give as he has decided in his heart, not reluctantly or under compulsion, for God loves a cheerful giver. And God is able to make all grace abound to you, so that having all sufficiency in all things at all times, you may abound in every good work."* (ESV)

What attitude should characterize our giving? What promise is given to the cheerful giver, and how does it relate to "every good work"? How does this passage encourage generous stewardship as a pathway to fulfilling purpose?

Now, also read **Matthew 6:19-21**:

> *"Do not lay up for yourselves treasures on earth, where moth and rust destroy and where thieves break in and steal, but lay up for yourselves treasures in heaven, where neither moth nor rust destroys and where thieves do not break in and steal. For where your treasure is, there your heart will be also."* (ESV)

What contrast does Jesus draw between earthly and heavenly treasures? Where does He say our "heart will be" in relation to our treasure? How does this teaching guide our perspective on accumulating wealth and possessions, and how does it relate to living purposefully for God's Kingdom?

Guided Reflection

Write down your reflections on the questions above and your insights from 2 Corinthians 9:7-8 and Matthew 6:19-21. Consider your current financial habits and use of possessions. What is one practical step you can take this week to more intentionally **steward your resources** for God's Kingdom, whether through giving, responsible spending, or wise saving?

Devotional: Using What We Have for Eternal Impact

Stewardship is a powerful expression of our trust in God and our commitment to His Kingdom. It's not just about tithing or giving financially, though those are important. It's about recognizing that every rand, every possession, every skill, and every opportunity is a tool God can use if we surrender it to Him. When we manage our resources wisely and generously, we become active participants in God's redemptive work, supporting ministries, aiding those in need, and investing in initiatives that bring about lasting change.

This week, take time to review your financial and material resources with a **Kingdom mindset**. Ask God to show you how you can use what you have to further His purposes. This might involve setting a budget that allows for generous giving, making intentional decisions about your purchases, or finding ways to use your possessions to bless others. Remember, even small acts of faithful stewardship can have significant eternal impact.

By entrusting our resources to God, we free ourselves from the anxieties of accumulation and step into the joy of participating in His abundant provision and eternal plans.

Prayer Prompt

Spend time in prayer thanking God for His provision and for entrusting you with resources. Pray for wisdom and discipline to be a faithful steward of everything you have. Ask for a generous heart that desires to use your resources for His Kingdom purposes and for the good of others.

Personal Reflection & Growth Journal

Significant Moments / Insights from This Week's Study

What happened? What was the insight?

_____

_____

_____

_____

_____

Emotional/Spiritual Responses:

_____
_____
_____
_____

Spiritual Insights/Lessons Learned:

- First thoughts:

_____
_____
_____
_____

- New perspectives gained:

_____
_____
_____
_____

- My Response/Action:

_____
_____
_____
_____

What helped me connect with God/grow this ?week?

_____
_____
_____
_____

What hindered my connection/?growth?

_____
_____
_____
_____

Week 48: Living with Endurance and Long-Term Vision

Fulfilling God's purpose for our lives is rarely a short-term sprint; it's a marathon that requires sustained effort, perseverance, and a steadfast gaze towards the future. A life of purpose is built day by day, choice by choice, often demanding endurance through periods of waiting, challenge, or seemingly small progress. Cultivating a long-term vision, grounded in God's faithfulness, enables us to remain steadfast, even when the immediate path is unclear.

Think about areas in your life where you've had to show remarkable endurance to achieve a goal. What kept you going? Reflect on any areas where you feel discouraged or impatient in your pursuit of purpose, and consider the role of a long-term perspective.

Scripture Prompt

Spend time meditating on **Hebrews 12:1-2**:

"Therefore, since we are surrounded by so great a cloud of witnesses, let us also lay aside every weight, and sin which clings so closely, and let us run with endurance the race that is set before us, looking to Jesus, the founder and perfecter of our faith, who for the joy that was set before him endured the cross, despising the shame, and is seated at the right hand of the throne of God." (ESV)

What imagery is used to describe the Christian life and our pursuit of purpose? What are we encouraged to "lay aside"? What is the central focus or model for our endurance? How does Jesus' own endurance inspire us to live with long-term vision?

Now, also read **Proverbs 29:18 (KJV or similar for "vision")**:

"Where there is no prophetic vision the people cast off restraint, but blessed is he who keeps the law." (ESJV or preferred translation like NASB "revelation")

While "prophetic vision" can mean direct revelation, it broadly speaks to a clear sense of divine purpose or direction. What is the consequence when there is no such vision? What positive outcome comes from holding onto and living by God's revealed will? How does a clear, long-term vision provide direction and guard against aimlessness?

Guided Reflection

Write down your reflections on the questions above and your insights from Hebrews 12:1-2 and Proverbs 29:18. Consider your personal purpose journey. What specific "weights or sins" might be hindering your endurance? What long-term vision for your life or your contribution to God's Kingdom keeps you motivated through challenges?

Devotional: The Steadfast Pursuit of Calling

Living with endurance means committing to God's calling even when results aren't immediately visible, or the path is arduous. It's understanding that growth, transformation, and impact often happen incrementally, not instantaneously. A long-term vision, rooted in God's unchanging character and promises, allows us to persist through setbacks, knowing that His timing is perfect and His ultimate plan will prevail. It liberates us from the tyranny of immediate gratification and anchors us in eternal significance.

This week, intentionally cultivate a spirit of endurance and a long-term vision. When you feel impatient or discouraged, remind yourself of God's faithfulness throughout history and in your own life. Re-read scriptures that speak to perseverance and God's ultimate victory. Identify one area where you need more endurance and focus on taking small, consistent steps forward, trusting that God is at work, even when you can't see the full picture.

Remember, the greatest impact often comes from sustained faithfulness. By running with endurance and holding onto God's vision, you are positioning yourself to fulfill the deep and lasting purposes He has for your life, contributing to His eternal Kingdom.

Prayer Prompt

Spend time in prayer asking God for strength and endurance to run the race He has set before you. Pray for a clear, long-term vision for your purpose that keeps you focused amidst distractions and challenges. Ask for patience and trust in His perfect timing.

Personal Reflection & Growth Journal

Significant Moments / Insights from This Week's Study

What happened? What was the insight?

_____

_____

_____

_____

_____

Emotional/Spiritual Responses:

_____

_____

_____

_____

_____

Spiritual Insights/Lessons Learned:

- First thoughts:

_____

_____

_____

_____

- New perspectives gained:

_____

_____

_____

_____

- My Response/Action:

_____

_____

_____

_____

What helped me connect with God/grow this ?week?

_____

_____

_____

_____

What hindered my connection/?growth?

_____

_____

_____

_____

Week 49: Leaving a Godly Legacy

As we journey through "Living with Purpose," we come to reflect on the lasting impact of our lives – the legacy we leave behind. A godly legacy isn't necessarily about fame or wealth, but about the enduring influence of our faith, character, and service on future generations and the world around us. It's about living in such a way that our purpose continues to bear fruit long after we are gone, sowing seeds of righteousness and truth that will bless others. In a land with a rich history and a vibrant future like South Africa, thinking about legacy connects us deeply to the past and our responsibility for what lies ahead.

Think about individuals who have left a positive, godly legacy in your life or in history. What characteristics defined their impact? Reflect on what kind of spiritual, relational, or societal impact you hope to leave, guided by your faith.

Scripture Prompt

Spend time meditating on **Psalm 78:4**:

> *"We will not hide them from their children, but tell to the coming generation the glorious deeds of the Lord, and his might, and the wonders that he has done."* (ESV)

What is the responsibility of one generation towards the next? What specific "deeds of the Lord" are meant to be passed on? How does this verse highlight the intergenerational aspect of godly legacy?

Now, also read **Hebrews 11:4**:

> *"By faith Abel offered to God a more acceptable sacrifice than Cain, through which he was commended as righteous, God commending him by accepting his gifts. And through his faith, though he died, he still speaks."* (ESV)

What was the defining characteristic of Abel's life and offering? How did his faith continue to "speak" even after his death? What does this imply about the lasting power of a life lived by faith, regardless of its length or public recognition?

Guided Reflection

Reflect on the questions above and your insights from Psalm 78:4 and Hebrews 11:4. Consider the spheres of influence God has given you (family, friends, workplace, community). What specific spiritual truths, values, or acts of service do you want to intentionally cultivate and pass on to those who come after you?

Devotional: Living with Tomorrow in Mind

A godly legacy is built not by grand plans alone, but by consistent, faithful living in the present. It's woven into the fabric of our daily choices: the words we speak, the integrity we uphold, the love we show, the compassion we extend, and the wisdom we share. It's about investing in people and principles that outlast us, understanding that our purpose has an eternal dimension. The impact we have often ripples far beyond what we can immediately see or measure.

This week, approach your days with an awareness of the legacy you are building. Consider how your actions and choices today might influence tomorrow. This could involve mentoring someone younger, investing in a cause that promotes justice, teaching biblical truths to your children or spiritual children, or simply living with such authentic faith that it inspires others. Think about the values you want to be remembered for and actively seek to embody them.

Remember, every life lived for Christ leaves a lasting imprint. By intentionally pursuing God's purpose and faithfully stewarding the influence He gives us, we contribute to a legacy that glorifies Him and blesses generations to come.

Prayer Prompt

Spend time in prayer asking God to help you live with an eternal perspective and to build a godly legacy. Pray for wisdom to know how to invest your life in ways that will have lasting spiritual impact. Ask for a heart that desires to bless future generations and to reflect Christ's enduring love through your life.

Personal Reflection & Growth Journal

Significant Moments / Insights from This Week's Study

What happened? What was the insight?

_____

_____

_____

_____

_____

Emotional/Spiritual Responses:

_____

_____

_____

_____

_____

Spiritual Insights/Lessons Learned:

- First thoughts:

_____

_____

_____

_____

- New perspectives gained:

_____

_____

_____

_____

- My Response/Action:

_____

_____

_____

_____

What helped me connect with God/grow this ?week?

_____

_____

_____

_____

What hindered my connection/?growth?

_____

_____

_____

_____

Week 50: Embracing Continuous Growth and Future Purpose

As we draw closer to the end of our annual journey, it's crucial to understand that living with purpose is not a destination we arrive at and then cease to develop. Instead, it is a dynamic, lifelong process of continuous growth, adaptation, and discovery. God's calling unfolds in seasons, often revealing new facets of our purpose as we mature in faith and experience. Embracing this ongoing journey allows us to remain flexible, open to His leading, and ready for the next steps in our purposeful lives, much like how the landscapes around us change with the seasons, revealing new beauty.

Think about how you have grown and changed over the past year, or even over your lifetime. What new understandings or challenges have shaped your path? Reflect on the idea that God's purpose for you might evolve and expand.

Scripture Prompt

Spend time meditating on **Philippians 3:13-14**:

> *"Brothers, I do not consider that I have made it my own. But one thing I do: forgetting what lies behind and straining forward to what lies ahead, I press on toward the goal for the prize of the upward call of God in Christ Jesus."* (ESV)

What attitude does Paul express about his past accomplishments or failures? What is his singular focus? How does this verse encourage a forward-looking perspective in our pursuit of purpose, rather than dwelling on the past?

Now, also read **Proverbs 16:9**:

> *"The heart of man plans his way, but the Lord establishes his steps."* (ESV)

What does this proverb say about human planning? What is God's role in our journey and plans? How does acknowledging God's sovereignty encourage both our active planning and our openness to His divine redirection in our purpose?

Guided Reflection

Reflect on the questions above and your insights from Philippians 3:13-14 and Proverbs 16:9. Consider an area of your life where you sense a need for continued growth. What new skills, knowledge, or spiritual disciplines might God be inviting you to explore for future purpose?

Devotional: The Unfolding Tapestry of God's Plan

God's purpose for us is often like a tapestry, where each thread of our past, present, and future is intricately woven together. We may only see a small section at a time, but with each new season and every step of growth, more of the beautiful design is revealed. Embracing continuous growth means maintaining a posture of learning, humility, and responsiveness to the Holy Spirit. It means being willing to adapt, to shed old ways of thinking, and to step into new challenges as God leads.

This week, intentionally reflect on the journey you've taken so far this year. What lessons have you learned? What new strengths have you discovered? As you look forward, hold your plans loosely, trusting that God is establishing your steps. Be open to new opportunities for service, learning, or contribution that may not fit your current expectations.

Remember, the God who began a good work in you will carry it on to completion (Philippians 1:6). Your purpose is an unfolding story, and each step of growth prepares you for the next chapter of living a life fully devoted to Him.

Prayer Prompt

Spend time in prayer thanking God for the journey of growth and purpose. Pray for a heart that is eager to learn and adapt, and for open hands to receive whatever new assignments or opportunities He has for you. Ask for clarity and boldness as you step into the next season of His unfolding plan for your life.

Personal Reflection & Growth Journal

Significant Moments / Insights from This Week's Study

What happened? What was the insight?

_____

_____

_____

_____

_____

Emotional/Spiritual Responses:

_____

_____

_____

_____

_____

Spiritual Insights/Lessons Learned:

- First thoughts:

_____

_____

_____

_____

- New perspectives gained:

_____

_____

_____

_____

- My Response/Action:

_____

_____

_____

_____

What helped me connect with God/grow this ?week?

_____

_____

_____

_____

What hindered my connection/?growth?

_____

_____

_____

_____

Week 51: Gratitude and Celebration in Purpose

As we approach the culmination of our annual journey, it's vital to pause and cultivate a spirit of **gratitude** and **celebration** in our purposeful living. True purpose isn't just about striving; it's also about acknowledging God's faithfulness in our lives and His work through us. Taking time to celebrate milestones, no matter how small, and to express heartfelt thanks for His guidance and provision, strengthens our faith and energises us for the path ahead. This practice allows us to truly appreciate the beauty of the journey and the blessings along the way.

Think back over the entire year of this devotional journey. What are some specific instances where you've seen God's hand at work in your life? What achievements, insights, or moments of growth are you particularly grateful for?

Scripture Prompt

Spend time meditating on **Psalm 100:4-5**:

> *"Enter his gates with thanksgiving, and his courts with praise! Give thanks to him; bless his name! For the Lord is good; his steadfast love endures forever, and his faithfulness to all generations."* (ESV)

What actions are we encouraged to take when approaching God? What are the specific reasons given for giving thanks and praise? How does remembering God's goodness, steadfast love, and faithfulness encourage a spirit of gratitude in our purposeful lives?

Now, also read **1 Thessalonians 5:18**:

> *"give thanks in all circumstances; for this is the will of God in Christ Jesus for you."* (ESV)

What is the scope of this instruction regarding thanksgiving? What significant statement is made about its importance? How does practicing gratitude in *all* circumstances, even challenges, align with fulfilling God's will and purpose?

Guided Reflection

Write down your reflections on the questions above and your insights from Psalm 100:4-5 and 1 Thessalonians 5:18. Identify three specific things you are grateful for from this past year related to your purpose, growth, or connections with others. How can you intentionally celebrate or express this gratitude to God and to others this week?

Devotional: The Power of a Thankful Heart

Gratitude shifts our perspective from what is lacking to what has been given. Celebration allows us to acknowledge God's active presence and power in our lives, reinforcing our trust in Him for the future. In our pursuit of purpose, it's easy to focus only on what's next, or what still needs to be done. However, pausing to express thanks and celebrate empowers us, deepens our joy, and confirms that our efforts are not in vain, but are part of a larger, divinely orchestrated plan.

This week, intentionally practice gratitude. Keep a gratitude journal, listing specific blessings related to your purposeful journey. Take time to verbally thank God for His guidance. Share stories of His faithfulness with trusted friends or family. Consider a small, personal celebration for a milestone reached or a challenge overcome. This isn't about pride, but about recognizing God's grace at work in and through you.

Remember, a thankful heart is a magnet for more blessings. By embracing gratitude and celebration, you not only honor God but also cultivate a spirit of joy that sustains you in your ongoing pursuit of His purpose.

Prayer Prompt

Spend time in prayer expressing deep gratitude to God for His faithfulness throughout the year and for the purpose He has revealed in your life. Thank Him for specific ways He has led, provided, and used you. Pray for a heart that is always quick to give thanks and to celebrate His goodness.

Personal Reflection & Growth Journal

Significant Moments / Insights from This Week's Study

What happened? What was the insight?

_____

_____

_____

_____

_____

Emotional/Spiritual Responses:

_____

_____

_____

_____

_____

Spiritual Insights/Lessons Learned:

- First thoughts:

_____
_____
_____
_____

- New perspectives gained:

_____
_____
_____
_____

- My Response/Action:

_____
_____
_____
_____

What helped me connect with God/grow this ?week?

_____
_____
_____
_____
_____

What hindered my connection/?growth?

_____
_____
_____
_____
_____

Week 52: Annual Review and Looking Ahead

This week marks the culmination of our year-long devotional journey. We've explored God's unchanging nature, the practical application of our faith in daily life, the beauty of connecting with others, and the profound journey of discovering and fulfilling God's purpose. This final week is a dedicated time for holistic review, to celebrate God's faithfulness throughout the entire year, and to prayerfully look ahead to what He has in store. It's a chance to consolidate your learnings and consider how you'll continue to walk in a deeper relationship with Him in the coming year.

Think back over the past 51 weeks. What was the most significant spiritual insight you gained? How has your understanding of God, yourself, and your relationships evolved? What are you most grateful for as you reflect on this journey?

Scripture Prompt

Spend time meditating on **Psalm 90:12**:

> *"So teach us to number our days that we may get a heart of wisdom."* (ESV)

What does "numbering our days" imply about our approach to time? What is the desired outcome of this practice? How does reflecting on the past year, in light of this verse, contribute to gaining a "heart of wisdom" for the future?

Now, also read **Philippians 1:6**:

> *"And I am sure of this, that he who began a good work in you will bring it to completion at the day of Jesus Christ."* (ESV)

What assurance does this verse offer regarding God's work in your life? What does it mean that God will "bring it to completion"? How does this promise empower you as you look ahead to continuous growth and purpose in the coming year?

Guided Reflection

Write down your reflections on the questions above and your insights from Psalm 90:12 and Philippians 1:6. Take time to review your journal entries from throughout the year. Consider the following:

- What are the top three spiritual truths or practices that had the most significant impact on you this year?

- In what specific area(s) of your life (e.g., relationship with God, living out faith, connecting with others, purpose) did you experience the most growth?

- What is one area you feel God is highlighting for continued focus and deeper spiritual growth in the upcoming year?

- As you look ahead, what specific prayer or intention do you want to carry with you into the new year, trusting God's faithfulness?

Devotional: A Year of Grace, A Future of Promise

Completing a year-long journey like this is a testament to God's grace and your perseverance. It's a moment to acknowledge how far you've come, the lessons you've learned, and the ways God has faithfully met you in each week's exploration. The purpose of this final review isn't just to reminisce, but to solidify the foundations laid and to anticipate the ongoing work of God in your life.

As you step into a new season, remember that God's work in you is continuous. He is not done shaping you, revealing Himself to you, or using you for His Kingdom purposes. Approach the coming year with a sense of anticipation, a heart open to His leading, and a commitment to applying the truths you've learned. Carry forward the disciplines that have brought you closer to Him and be willing to embrace new challenges and opportunities for growth.

May this review be a moment of deep gratitude, renewed commitment, and joyful expectation for all that God will do in and through you in the days ahead.

Prayer Prompt

Spend time in prayer, offering a heartfelt prayer of thanks to God for His faithfulness throughout this entire year. Confess any areas where you fell short and ask for His grace for the future. Pray for wisdom, clarity, and a deeper walk with Him in the year to come, surrendering your plans to His perfect will.

Personal Reflection & Growth Journal

Significant Moments / Insights from This Week's Study

What happened? What was the insight?

_____

_____

_____

_____

_____

Emotional/Spiritual Responses:

_____

_____

_____

Spiritual Insights/Lessons Learned:

- First thoughts:

_____

_____

_____

_____

- New perspectives gained:

_____

_____

_____

_____

- My Response/Action:

_____

_____

_____

_____

What helped me connect with God/grow this ?week?

_____

_____

_____

_____

What hindered my connection/?growth?

_____

_____

_____

_____

Conclusion: A Journey of Faith, Growth, and Purpose

As we draw this year-long devotional journey to a close, we stand at a threshold, looking back at the ground we've covered and forward to the path ahead. It has been a privilege to walk through the foundational truths of God's character, the practical expressions of our faith, the richness of our connections with others, and the profound calling to live a life of purpose.

This guide was designed not just for reading, but for *living*. We've explored how a deeper understanding of **God's nature** (Quarter 1) transforms our worship, our trust, and our very identity. We then moved into **living out our faith** (Quarter 2), tackling practical applications in areas like forgiveness, patience, and managing our thoughts and words. Our journey continued into **connecting with others** (Quarter 3), emphasizing the beauty and challenge of community, relationships, and extending grace. Finally, we delved into **living with purpose** (Quarter 4), understanding our unique calling, stewarding our gifts, and leaving a godly legacy.

The true fruit of this journey lies not just in the pages filled, but in the heart transformed. It's in the quiet moments of prayer where God spoke, the challenging situations where you chose to act in faith, the relationships that deepened, and the new ways you discovered to serve.

Remember, the spiritual life is a continuous unfolding. The God who faithfully guided you through these 52 weeks is the same God who promises to be with you always, teaching, equipping, and empowering you for every step of your ongoing journey. May the insights gained, the habits formed, and the truths embraced become deeply embedded in your life, propelling you forward with greater **wisdom, love, and purpose**.

As you step into what lies ahead, carry with you the assurance that you are deeply loved, uniquely gifted, and eternally purposed by the Living God. Continue to seek His face, listen for His voice, and walk in obedience, knowing that His plan for you is good, perfect, and will bring Him glory.

May your life be a testament to His faithfulness.

Journal Pages

JOURNAL

JOURNAL

JOURNAL

JOURNAL

JOURNAL

Check out another book in the series

Welcome Aboard, Check Out This Limited-Time Free Bonus!

Ahoy, reader! Welcome to the Ahoy Publications family, and thanks for snagging a copy of this book! Since you've chosen to join us on this journey, we'd like to offer you something special.

Check out the link below for a FREE e-book filled with delightful facts about American History.

But that's not all - you'll also have access to our exclusive email list with even more free e-books and insider knowledge. Well, what are ye waiting for? Click the link below to join and set sail toward exciting adventures in American History.

Access your bonus here
https://ahoypublications.com/
Or, Scan the QR code!

References

10 Best Psalms About Trusting God (And Not the World). (2020, November 15). Psalm 91. https://psalm91.com/2020/11/15/10-best-psalms-about-trusting-god-and-not-the-world/

10 Psalms of Trust in God's Goodness and Care for His People – BibleTruths. (2017, November 22). BibleTruths. https://www.bibletruths.org/10-psalms-trust-god-goodness-care/

Anderson, E. (2024, July 12). 5 Themes From the Psalms – The Rebelution. The Rebelution. https://www.therebelution.com/blog/2024/07/5-themes-from-the-psalms/

Brodie, J. (2020, October 26). 6 Beautiful Psalms for Encouragement for You in Your Daily Life. Christianity.com; Salem Web Network. https://www.christianity.com/wiki/bible/psalms-to-encourage-you-in-your-daily-life.html

Bucher, M. (2018, November 3). Who Was Mary Magdalene in the Bible? – 5 Questions Answered. Bible Study Tools; Salem Web Network. https://www.biblestudytools.com/bible-study/topical-studies/who-was-mary-magdalene.html

Carroll, J. (2006, June). Who Was Mary Magdalene? Smithsonian; Smithsonian.com. https://www.smithsonianmag.com/history/who-was-mary-magdalene-119565482/

Fr. Stavros Akrotirianakis. (2020, April 28). Psalm 11—Trusting in God Must Be a Consistent Theme. Orthodox Christian Network. https://myocn.net/psalm-11-trusting-in-god-must-be-a-consistent-theme/

Guiley, R. E. (2021, December 7). The Importance of Prayer and Meditation. Unity.org. https://www.unity.org/article/importance-prayer-and-meditation

Lucey, C. (2020, December 29). Who Was Mary the Mother of Jesus? Christianity.com. https://www.christianity.com/wiki/holidays/who-was-mary-the-mother-of-jesus.html

The Role of Psalms in Christian Worship. (2024, June 5). Digital Bible; Digital Bible. https://digitalbible.ca/article-page/modern-topics-what-does-the-bible-say-about-psalm

WHN. (2010, December 26). Mary, Mother of Jesus Christ. Women's History Network. https://womenshistorynetwork.org/mary-mother-of-jesus-christ/

Worshiping with the Psalms. (2015). Reformed Worship. https://www.reformedworship.org/article/june-2016/worshiping-psalms

Image Sources

1 https://www.pexels.com/photo/person-holding-brown-holy-bible-5199796/

2 designed by Freepik. https://www.freepik.com/free-photo/words-smart-goals-with-dart-target-dartboard_1131515.htm

3 https://www.pexels.com/photo/close-up-shot-of-a-person-reading-a-bible-5206052/

4 https://www.pexels.com/photo/close-up-photo-of-bible-4654082/

5 https://www.pexels.com/photo/silhouette-of-man-with-angel-wings-during-dawn-2043837/

6 designed by Freepik. https://www.freepik.com/free-vector/gradient-ascension-day-illustration_25001742.htm

7 https://www.pexels.com/photo/rosary-on-holy-bible-5875398/

8 https://www.pexels.com/photo/close-up-of-the-bible-5124915/

9 designed by Freepik. https://www.freepik.com/free-vector/hand-drawn-moses-illustration_37370323.htm

10 designed by Freepik. https://www.freepik.com/free-photo/front-view-person-making-heart-from-holy-book-pages_9469595.htm

11 designed by Freepik. https://www.freepik.com/free-photo/vertical-shot-female-wearing-biblical-robe-with-her-hands-up-towards-sky-praying_8981177.htm

12 designed by Freepik. https://www.freepik.com/free-photo/portrait-queen-with-royal-crown_40391193.htm

13 https://www.pexels.com/photo/writing-typography-blur-bokeh-11506026/

14 https://www.pexels.com/photo/a-man-in-brown-robe-holding-a-shepherd-s-crook-7360551/

15 https://www.pexels.com/photo/waterfall-in-mountainous-terrain-with-steep-slopes-5668668/

16 https://www.pexels.com/photo/open-bible-book-lying-on-white-blanket-among-decorations-

22711043/

17 https://www.pexels.com/photo/silhouette-image-of-person-praying-1615776/

18 https://www.pexels.com/photo/sheep-grazing-on-dramatic-cliff-edge-28544171/

19 designed by Freepik. https://www.freepik.com/free-photo/person-wearing-biblical-robe-standing-water-with-blurred_14256138.htm

20 https://www.pexels.com/photo/new-testament-book-5421124/

21 designed by Freepik. https://www.freepik.com/free-photo/shallow-focus-shot-jesus-christ-giving-piece-bread-female-wearing-biblical-robe_13291250.htm

22 https://www.pexels.com/photo/mother-mary-and-christ-figurine-on-black-background-51524/

23 https://www.pexels.com/photo/colorful-cutouts-of-the-word-purpose-4116640/

24 https://www.pexels.com/photo/ancient-wall-decoration-5624531/

25 https://www.pexels.com/photo/shallow-focus-of-sprout-401213/

26 https://www.pexels.com/photo/woman-wearing-white-long-sleeved-shirt-prayng-3285947/

27 designed by Freepik. https://www.freepik.com/free-photo/close-up-priest-talking-with-person_22814903.htm